Jon Gough
5/2000
(from Rick
Spalding)

D0980980

The Preaching Life

The Preaching Life

Barbara Brown Taylor

COWLEY PUBLICATIONS
Cambridge ✦ Boston
Massachusetts

Published in the United States of America by Cowley Publications, a division of the Society of St. John the Evangelist. No portion of this book may be reproduced, stored in or introduced into a retrieval system, or transmitted, in any form or by any means—including photocopying—without the prior written permission of Cowley Publications, except in the case of brief quotations embodied in critical articles and reviews.

Cover Illustration: *Twilight in the Wilderness* (Detail), oil on canvas, 1860, Frederic Edwin Church, American
© The Cleveland Museum of Art, Mr. and Mrs. William H. Marlatt Fund, 65.233

International Standard Book Number: 1-56101-074-X
Library of Congress Number: 92-34743

All quotations are from the New Revised Standard Version of the Bible unless otherwise indicated.

Library of Congress Cataloging-in-Publication Data
Taylor, Barbara Brown.
    The preaching life / Barbara Brown Taylor
        p. cm.
ISBN 1-56101-074-X
    1. Taylor, Barbara Brown. 2. Episcopal Church—Clergy—Biography. 3. Anglican Communion—United States—Clergy—Biography. 4. Episcopal Church—Sermons. 5. Anglican Communion—Sermons. 6. Sermons, American. I. Title.
BX5995.T26A3 1993
283'.092—dc20   92-34743

This book is printed on acid-free paper and was produced in the United States of America.

Seventh printing

Cowley Publications
28 Temple Place
Boston, Massachusetts 02111

for Grace and Earl,

givers of life

Acknowledgments

I am grateful to many people for their parts in the creation of this book:

Lynn Wehr, my friend and helper, who held my hand as I approached a computer for the first time and initiated me into the mysteries of WordPerfect 5.1;

Cynthia Shattuck, my gifted editor, whose generous companionship has meant as much to me as her clarity of vision and sense of purpose;

Fred Craddock, my guide, who changed the way I heard the good news and made me want to preach it too, and whose gentle encouragement has strengthened my spirit;

The people of All Saints' Church, Atlanta, and Grace-Calvary Church, Clarkesville, my fellow travelers, who have listened, and by listening well, have shaped the life of this preacher;

Harry Pritchett, Ann Woodall, Judy Barber, Mary Ann Bowman, Mary Foster, Carol Pepper, Peter Hawkins, Bill Swift and Martha Sterne, my allies and advocates, whose belief in the power of the word has kept my engine running;

and Edward Taylor, my husband, whose steadfast love and uncomplaining support have taught me what gospel is all about.

Table of Contents

Foreword

by Fred B. Craddock

To introduce you to this book is to introduce you to Barbara Brown Taylor. She has that rare capacity to sit on her own shoulder and report on what she sees and hears herself doing and saying. She talks about what she does and then does what she talks about. One is reminded of Somerset Maugham's *The Summing Up* and Annie Dillard's *The Writing Life*. But one is reminded also of oneself, of what it is like to trust and to doubt at the same time, to be inside and outside at the same time, to run from and to run toward at the same time, to love an activity more than anything and at the same time welcome every chance to be free of it. As for introducing Barbara, what can I say that will not rob you of the serious pleasure of making your own discoveries?

Is Barbara Brown Taylor primarily a preacher? No. To be sure, she preaches every Sunday in her parish and in parishes around the country, and she does it extremely well. Ask her parishioners, ask other clergy who invite her into their pulpits, or better yet, read the sermons in this book. You will not simply be reading; you will be hearing. Few can excel Barbara in writing to be heard as well as to be read. She will lead you in and out of biblical texts, great literature, and life itself. And she will do so with realism. These sermons are not make believe; she knows that faith is high risk and that the signs of hope in our world are as a small sprout on an old stump. Barbara understands how fragile and vulnerable a sermon seems, tossed as a seed which even the birds can take away. Because she knows the struggle of faith against great odds, Barbara is the right preacher for the audience Bill Muehl describes in *Why Preach? Why Listen?* as those who "almost didn't come this morning." Even so, she is not primarily a preacher.

Is Barbara primarily a teacher? No. She teaches, to be sure, and she does so widely, and well. Invitations to seminaries, workships, and pastors' conferences are far more than she can accept. I know why: we have teamed together on many occasions with ministers gathered around the subject of preaching. She holds up the pulpit there as she does in this book. Her instruction is to the benefit of all, whether they be beginning ministry and fear the pulpit or experienced and capable but seeking to improve, or tired and jaded and feeling the unrelenting regularity of Sundays. As you will see so clearly in this volume, she reminds us all about the gift of words, what they do, and how they fit together in ways that change both listener and speaker. But Barbara is not primarily a teacher.

Barbara Brown Taylor is primarily a worshiper. Whether in the study, in a classroom, in a hospital room, on a mountain trail, or in the pulpit, she is in the sanctuary. You will find an altar in every paragraph of this book. The offering of the right word, the appropriate word, is not solely to the reader: it is to God. She works with God's word, God's people, God's gifts, God's hope for the world. Read this book and you will be standing beside her, before God.

So come on in. You who are entering ministry and wonder what it is like inside, come on in. You who are ministers who have forgotten your call and those trembling beginnings, come on in. And you who are not ministers but who are standing on the porch, unsure of whether you are seeking or being sought, come on in. You will be completely free after the last page to go or to stay.

Fred B. Craddock
Emory University
Atlanta

Part One

The
Life
of
Faith

CHAPTER ONE

A Church in Ruins

T wo summers ago, I traveled to northeastern Turkey for a walk in the Kachkar Mountains, a stretch of land between the Black and Caspian seas where the kingdom of Georgia flourished during the eleventh and twelfth centuries. During its brief ascendance in this part of the world, Georgia was a kind of Camelot, a Christian kingdom in which strong and benevolent rulers carved a culture out of the wilderness and defended it from its enemies. They imported Byzantine artists from Constantinople to adorn their public buildings, and built an economy that prospered all their subjects. Two hundred years later it was all gone, torn to pieces by neighboring tribes. Now it is a wilderness again, although a beautiful one—a kingdom of mountains, tall pines, and rushing streams populated only by the handful of people who have found flat places to farm.

One afternoon in the middle of nowhere, a guide led a group of trekkers up a dirt road toward a small settlement hidden behind some trees. We turned a bend and the outline of a ruined cathedral appeared, a huge gray stone church with a central dome that dominated the countryside. Grass grew between what was left of the roof tiles and the facade was crumbling, but even in shambles, it spoke to us. The whole group fell silent before it, looking around for permission to enter, but no permission was necessary. It was a hull, a shell. No living thing remained inside, and we were free to explore.

Arriving at the main portal, I stepped through and was swallowed up by the sheer size of the space inside. Very little of the roof had survived, but the massive walls still held plaster frescoes with the shadows of biblical scenes on them. There were lambs of God carved on the stone capitals and medieval saints with their faces chipped away. Some of the best stones had been plundered for other purposes, but those that remained testified to the care and expense that had been lavished on this house of God.

Poking around, I found evidence of campfires in one side chapel. The other had been turned into a garbage dump, where rats prowled for scraps. From the transept I heard the sound of children and returned to find them playing soccer on the green lawn that covered the floor of the central nave, while a couple of sheep grazed under the apse. In the dome just above, it was still possible to see one outstretched arm of the Pantocrator who had presided over the eucharist; the rest of him had flaked away. Sitting down under what was left of his embrace, I surveyed the ruins of his church.

It is one thing to talk about the post-Christian era and quite another to walk around inside it. Christianity died in Turkey—the land that gave birth to Paul and that he found so fertile for the sowing of his gospel—the land of Ephesus, Galatia, Colossae, Nicaea. The last Armenian baptisms were recorded as late as the 1890s, but today the Christian population of Turkey is less than one percent of the total. Churches that were the jewels of Byzantine Christendom have been stripped of their altars, fonts, and crosses. Many have been turned into mosques while others are open to tourists as museums and still others have been left to rot. Looking around that magnificent Georgian cathedral that had been abandoned for almost a thousand years, I imagined my own parish in its place: the beautiful wooden rafters rotted out and the ceiling collapsed, shards of stained glass hanging from the windowpanes, the carved stone altar removed to some museum along with the processional cross—vestiges of an ancient faith no longer practiced in the land.

Such a thing is not impossible; that is what I learned in that ruin on the hillside. God has given us good news in human form and has even given us the grace to proclaim it, but part of our terrible freedom is the freedom to lose our voices, to forget where we were going and why. While that knowledge does not yet strike me as prophetic, it does keep me from taking both my own ministry and the ministry of the whole church for granted. If we do not attend to God's presence in our midst and bring all our best gifts to serving that presence in the world, we may find ourselves selling tickets to a museum.

As best I can figure, the Christian era ended during my lifetime. When I was eight years old in small-town Alabama, there was nothing to do on Sundays but to go to church. Everything else was closed, because decent people both observed the Sabbath and removed temptation from those who did not. All my friends wore mustard seed necklaces and most of us owned child-sized New Testaments bound in white leatherette, given to us by our parents at Easter. In school we prayed to God as routinely as we pledged allegiance to the flag, and we memorized the Ten Commandments alongside our multiplication tables.

By the time I reached high school, God was dead. Pictures of Kent State and the My Lai massacre were tattooed on people's minds, and they turned their outrage on what they had been taught about God. God was not good. God did not answer prayer. God, for all practical purposes, was dead. All bets were off. Human beings were free to construct their own realities from any materials at hand and to express themselves any way they pleased. When lightning did not strike, their confidence grew along with their fear: that perhaps they really were alone in the universe after all.

5

Organized religion remained one of the many choices available to human beings in their search for meaning, but it was a lame one. On the college campus where I spent the early seventies, my peers let me know that only the un-imaginative still went to church—the stuck, the fearful, the socially inept—while those with any sense committed them-selves to more relevant causes, like the anti-war movement, or the environment, or the arts. Church-like communities formed around such causes, giving their members identity, purpose, and support. They had their own ideologies and codes of behavior as rigid as those of any religion, but no one seemed to notice. We gave our allegiance freely; it was not required of us, and whom we gave it to was each other.

Those with a spiritual bent sought revelations of God out-side the Christian tradition, allying themselves with Krishna, Meher Baba or Bahaullah, while others practiced transcendental meditation as faithfully as monks. From time to time, evangelical groups like the Navigators or Campus Crusade for Christ would launch offensives, sending teams of healthy, clean-cut young people to infiltrate the counter-cultural ranks. We never knew where they came from. They were our age but they were not students; they spoke English but they did not speak our language, using hard words with lots of consonants like "sacrifice," "conviction," and "hell."

A few of us bounced between both extremes and landed at the university chapel, where we found a kind of refuge from the chaos outside. It looked like a church. It smelled like a church. It had pews and candles, an altar and a cross, but we were as likely to hear a rock concert on Sunday morning as a sermon, and the prayers encompassed every cause on God's green earth. All of us who sat there barefoot in our embroidered blue jeans got the message: Jesus had dropped his requirements. It was no longer necessary for us to pretend to be something we were not in order to win his attention. He would come to us on his own, and he would come to us where we were.

The curriculum in the religion department told us the same thing. While courses in Bible and church history continued to be listed, they fell into the cracks between brave new offerings: feminist theology, liberation theology, theology and ecology. The tables had turned. The old theology that placed humankind in the service of God had failed; the world was still a mess. The new theology placed God in the service of humankind; perhaps we would do better. But if the tables had turned, only a few of us sat at them. Religion majors were a rare breed in the seventies. Students who wanted to make a real contribution prepared for law or medical school, not seminary, while the rest enrolled in business school. They might not change the world, but at least they would be able to pay their bills.

That was almost twenty years ago, and while there must be a dozen different explanations for what went on in those days, the trend has continued. Faith in God is no longer the rule; it is the exception to the rule, one "option" among many for people seeking to make sense out of their lives. A large number of them have been so wounded by their religious training that belief in God is too painful to consider. Not long ago I heard a mother defend her grown daughter's ignorance of Christianity. She herself had been schooled in a French Canadian convent, where nuns had bullied her for years in the name of God. When she escaped them, she vowed to protect her own children. "My daughter doesn't know Moses from Goliath," she says with some pride, "but at least she grew up without guilt."

Others feel betrayed by a God whom they believe to have broken an implicit promise. According to their Sunday school teachers, God made a bargain with each one of them the moment they were born: do what I say and I will take care of you. So they did, and for years it seemed to work. They obeyed their parents, their teachers, their coaches, and they were taken care of, but one day the system failed. They did everything right and everything went wrong. Their prayers went unanswered, their belief went unrewarded, their God went AWOL, and the lie was exposed. One man I know, mourning the death of his infant daughter, confessed the depth of his loss. "I don't know what to believe anymore," he said. "I don't know whom to pray to, or what to pray. I tried to be a good person; I did the best I knew how, and it didn't do a bit of good. If God is going to let something like this happen, then what's the use of believing at all?"

His disillusionment is emblematic of the post-Christian era, when the perceived promises of Christendom lie broken and the existence of God—never mind the omnipotence of God—seems a fantasy. Television evangelists are indicted for fraud and parish priests for child molestation; churches pour their resources into institutional survival while their numbers dwindle; religious wars are waged around the world while children's bellies bloat and whole species disappear off the face of the earth. These are grim times, in which the God of our fondest dreams is nowhere to be found.

But down in the darkness below those dreams—in the place where all our notions about God have come to naught—there is still reason to hope, because disillusionment is not so bad. Disillusionment is the loss of illusion—about ourselves, about the world, about God—and while it is almost always painful, it is not a bad thing to lose the lies we have mistaken for the truth. Disillusioned, we come to understand that God does not conform to our expectations. We glimpse our own relative size in the universe and see that no human being can say who God should be or how God should act. We review our requirements of God and recognize them as our own fictions, our own frail shelters against the vast night sky. Disillusioned, we find out what is not true and are set free to seek what is—if we dare.

Many of the disillusioned do not have the heart to pursue such freedom. The pain of their loss is too great. They have been robbed of the God who was supposed to be, and their fear of the God who might be makes it impossible for them to move. Anger becomes their best defense—anger at the hardness of their lives, anger at those who led them to expect more, anger at their own gullibility. Some are able to use their anger as a bridge back to God, but many more set their bridges on fire, denying the presence of God with all the fury of a rejected lover.

But there are also people who have let the idea of God go as easily as an old pair of shoes. They seem to be people who never expected much in the first place, who are so used to being let down—by parents, by friends, by life—that discarding their hopes comes as naturally to them as breathing. They learned early on that belief is nothing but a shortcut to disappointment, so they saved themselves the trouble, retiring belief in God along with belief in Santa Claus, Lady Luck, and the Tooth Fairy.

I say "they" but I also mean "we," because everyone who passes through the wilderness of disillusionment passes through these places where the wild beasts of wrath and resignation stalk their prey. There is a lot of attrition along the way, but for those who elect to go on the best advice is to keep moving. Putting one foot ahead of the other is the best way to survive disillusionment, because the real danger is not the territory itself but getting stuck in it.

For those willing to keep heaving themselves toward the light, things can change. What has been lost gradually becomes less important than what is to be found. Curiosity pokes its green head up through the asphalt of grief, and fear of the unknown takes on an element of wonder as the disillusioned turn away from the God who was supposed to be in order to seek the God who is. Every letdown becomes a lesson and a lure. Did God fail to come when I called? Then perhaps God is not a minion. So who is God? Did God fail to punish my adversary? Then perhaps God is not a policeman. So who is God? Did God fail to make everything turn out all right? Then perhaps God is not a fixer. So who is God?

Over and over, my disappointments draw me deeper into the mystery of God's being and doing. Every time God declines to meet my expectations, another of my idols is exposed. Another curtain is drawn back so that I can see what I have propped up in God's place—no, that is not God, so who is God? It is the question of a lifetime, and the answers are never big enough or finished. Pushing past curtain after curtain, it becomes clear that the failure is not God's but my own, for having such a poor and stingy imagination. God is greater than my imagination, wiser than my wisdom, more dazzling than the universe, as present as the air I breathe and utterly beyond my control.

That is, in short, what makes me a Christian. As the creature of a God like that, I need a mediator, an advocate, a flesh-and-blood handle on the inscrutable mystery that gives birth to everything that is. While Jesus is, in his own way, just as inscrutable, he is enough like me to convince me that relationship with God is not only possible, but deeply desired by God, who wants me to believe that love is the wide net spread beneath the most dangerous of my days.

To believe that is an act of faith—not a one-time decision, but a daily and sometimes hourly choice to act as if that were true in spite of all evidence to the contrary. Sometimes it feels like pure make-believe. I read the weekend newspaper, full of stories about violence, addiction, corruption, disaster, and I wonder whom I am kidding. Or my own life begins to spring leaks and I lie awake in the middle of the night faint with fear. I want a safer world. I want a more competent God. Then I remember that God's power is not a controlling but a redeeming power—the power to raise the dead, including those who are destroying themselves—and the red blood of belief begins to return to my veins. I have faith. I lose faith. I find faith again, or faith finds me, but throughout it all I am grasped by the possibility that it is all true: I am in good hands; love girds the universe; God will have the last word.

Believing that, I interpret my life and the life of the world in a different way. What appear to be death throes may be the strenuous pangs of birth. Human grief may be the ax that breaks down the door of human isolation. That brown bird with the sweet song and yellow eyes may be an angel of God sent to rouse me from my self-absorption. Every moment of my life offers me a choice about how I will perceive it—as happenstance or revelation? As one more blind accident of time and space or as the veiled disclosure of a present and compassionate God? When all is said and done, faith may be nothing more than the assignment of holy meaning to events that others call random.

On one hand, this changed perspective is the most valuable gift in the world, with power to save souls and change lives, but on the other hand it is the most difficult to defend. There is no proof that it is true. On the contrary, life is full of evidence that it is *not* true, at least not to the naked eye. While fame and fortune deliver their instant rewards, faith sows its seeds much deeper down. Its roots may grow a long time in the dark before anything shows on the surface, and its leaves may be mistaken for crabgrass or thistle. When its fruit finally appears, there may not be much demand for it, since those who eat it do not become fat but thin, thin and somewhat daft by the standards of the world.

This is the food that the people of God have been given to live on. It is not what most of us would have ordered. It is nothing we can grow all by ourselves, and no one may stockpile it for his or her own use. Day by day by day we are given not what we want but what we need. Sometimes it is a feast and sometimes it is swept crumbs, but by faith we believe it is enough to sustain us, if only because it comes to us from the hand of God. Reaching out our own hands to accept it, we learn that it is not our food alone. It is also the food we are meant to share with the world, a hungry world that is nonetheless suspicious of our food, having been fed both junk and poison in the name of God.

That, it seems to me, is where we are at the edge of the twenty-first century—"we" being the church of God, the body of Christ on earth. In this age of a million choices, we are the remnant, the sometimes faithful, sometimes unfaithful family of a difficult and glorious God, called to seek and proclaim God's presence in a disillusioned world. It is a world that claims to have left us behind, along with dragons and maps of a flat earth, but meanwhile the human heart continues to hunt its true home. Today it is crystals and past-life readings; tomorrow it may be travel to Mars. Ours is a restless and impatient race, known for abandoning our saviors as quickly as we elect them for not saving us soon or well or often enough.

Those of us who call ourselves Christian belong to that race. We are fickle and flawed, but we are more than that because we believe in a God who believes in us. God looks at us and sees the best: sees beloved children, sees likely allies, sees able partners in the ongoing work of creation. In faith, we set out to see the same things in ourselves and to live into them, trusting God's vision of us more than we trust our own. This is the work of the church, not only for our own members but for the whole world, work that is more important now than it has ever been, and more difficult.

Because I am a preacher, it is through a preacher's eyes that I tend to see that work, but because I am a baptized Christian too, it is from that perspective I write. Either way, my job remains the same: to proclaim the good news of God in Christ and to celebrate the sacraments of God's presence in the world. Those two jobs are described as clearly in the baptismal vows as they are in the ordination vows, which gives all Christians a common vocation. Our job is to stand with one foot on earth and one in heaven, with the double vision that is the gift of faith, and to say out of our own experience that reality is not flat but deep, not opaque but transparent, not meaningless but shot full of grace for those with the least willingness to believe it is so.

That is our common call. It comes to each one of us in a different way, calling for the particular gifts of our particular lives, and each of us is free to respond or play deaf. But God never stops calling. Lay any life out for close inspection and the truth becomes clear. God called us from the womb and calls us still, the tireless shepherd who never stops calling us home.

CHAPTER TWO

Call

S ome of my favorite memories are not my own but my mother's. One of those dates from the early 1950s, when I was temporarily her only child, a willful three year old with a nonstop tongue. My parents and I lived in rural Kansas, in a tract house on an old cornfield where the west wind blew so hard that everything in the yard grew toward Missouri. We had one of the two basements on the block, into which the whole neighborhood fit on those stifling afternoons when the sky turned green and tornadoes twirled on the far horizon.

Behind our small home was a patio, a swing set, and a long view to the east, where a convent sat in the distance like an oasis in the broom grass. One evening, my mother says, she missed me in the house and found me out there, facing the convent and calling "Nino!" at the top of my lungs. No one knew who Nino was, least of all me, but for some time I called him every day at dusk, singing his name across the dark field with the west wind in my hair and the setting sun at my back. He was not an imaginary playmate, apparently, because he never answered my call. I played alone during the days that I called him at night, and after a while I gave up, accepting the company of a baby sister instead.

Now I know that *nino* means "little boy" in Spanish, but that does not explain anything, nor does the story require explanation. I remember it because it is true. We are born seekers, calling strange names into the darkness from our earliest days because we know we are not meant to be alone, and because we know that we await someone whom we cannot always see.

My upbringing—by a southern Methodist mother and a midwestern Roman Catholic father—was a contentedly secular one. Although my parents did present me for baptism in the pre-Vatican II Catholic Church as an infant, that medieval event proved so traumatic for them that we did not attend church for the next seven years and neither of my younger sisters was baptized until she was an adult. My mother's explanation is simple: "That priest took you out of my arms, going on and on about your sinfulness, my sinfulness, everybody's sinfulness, and I thought, 'This is all wrong.' You were the best thing I had ever done in my life, and I could not wait to get you out of there."

By the time I was seven and there were five of us, my parents decided to give the church another try. We had moved twice by then and were all feeling the need to sit still among people who were more stable than we. After the Roman Catholics, the Methodists were the next logical choice, and before long we had found a whole congregation of them— way out in the Ohio countryside, in a white frame church with a matching parsonage and apple trees in the yard. The pastor was a kind young man with no family of his own, who soon became a regular guest at our supper table. I grew to adore him. He was vital and funny and could catch an airborne fly with one hand. He listened to me when I talked and let me lead him on tours of my projects around the house. He seemed able, when he looked at me, to see a person and not only a child, and I loved him for it.

One Sunday he asked me to sit up close to the pulpit. He wanted me to hear his sermon, he said, and as I listened to him talk about the beauty of God's creation and our duty to be awed by it, all of a sudden I heard him telling the congregation about a little girl who kept tadpoles in a birdbath so that she could watch over them as they turned into frogs, and how her care for those creatures was part of God's care for the whole world.

It was as if someone had turned on all the lights—not only to hear myself spoken of in church, but to hear that my life was part of God's life, and that something as ordinary as a tadpole connected the two. My friend's words changed everything for me. I could no longer see myself or the least detail of my life in the same way again. When the service was over that day I walked out of it into a God-enchanted world, where I could not wait to find further clues to heaven on earth. Every leaf, every ant, every shiny rock called out to me—begging to be watched, to be listened to, to be handled and examined. I became a detective of divinity, collecting evidence of God's genius and admiring the tracks left for me to follow: locusts shedding their hard bodies for soft, new, winged ones; prickly pods of milkweed spilling silky white hair; lightning spinning webs of cold fire in the sky, as intricate as the veins in my own wrist. My friend taught me to believe that these were all words in the language of God, hieroglyphs given to puzzle and delight me even if I never cracked the code.

I was a willing student until the day I lost my teacher. At first all I knew was that something was wrong. Threat hung in the air as it had on those dark afternoons in Kansas, only this time it was not the weather. "Civil rights" had come to Ohio, a phrase that made adults talk loudly and lose their tempers. They chose sides and defended them; they wanted my friend to choose sides too, and he did. The doors of the church were open, he said. He would stand there to make sure they remained open, he said, so that is where they hung him—in effigy—a grotesque stuffed figure that bore no resemblance to my friend, swaying in the heat as he packed and left town.

That was when I began to understand that God's call was not only wonderful but also terrible, that the bright gleam I pursued through the woods and fields behind my house had another dimension I knew nothing about. It had sharp edges to it. It was capable of cutting deep, and those who reached out to grasp it had best be prepared to bleed.

We moved from Ohio soon after that and there was no more church for several years, until I went with some of my friends to the sixth grade confirmation class at an Episcopal church in Alabama. Everything that happened there on a Sunday morning galvanized me: the hymns, the confession of sin, the eucharistic prayer, and communion itself, which I watched from a distance with something between desire and fear. At twelve I took to organized religion like a pig to mud, which makes me wonder if puberty does not unlock some doors of the soul along with those of the body. What was happening to me physically was so amazing that I was open to mystery at every other level of my being as well, and what I wanted, I got.

While the word "liturgy" was not yet in my vocabulary, I knew that what we did in church and how we did it mattered. There was a depth and flow to the service that carried me along with it—in which I participated but which was bigger that I was—until finally it deposited me at the door of the church, blinking in the sunshine and feeling clean through and through. Clean: that is the word I remember using for worship. I left church feeling scrubbed and refreshed, as if someone who cared about me had seen me whole and bathed me. It was the same feeling I got while reading *The Princess and the Goblin*, then one of my favorite books, by George Macdonald. There was one scene in particular that captivated me, a scene in which the princess was led by her fairy godmother to a chamber deep in the earth, a room ringed with candles so that everything in it glowed like the moon, and there the godmother bathed the little girl, filling a deep tub with warm, scented water and handling the child tenderly until she was clean.

I read that scene over and over again; I loved how it haunted me. I could not get the light out of my mind, or the warmth of the water, or the smell of the girl's clean skin after her godmother had toweled her off. It reminded me of my Grandma Lucy, my mother's mother, who died when I was seven. A local character in her hometown of College Park, Georgia, Grandma Lucy ran a boarding house on Main Street and threw her considerable weight around with aplomb. She was known both for her shrewd business sense and her bad temper, a combination that earned her a fair measure of respect in the community. In her later years she was an awesome presence, especially to a child. Having lost both legs to a case of diabetes she refused to treat, she presided from a stainless steel wheelchair, her two wooden legs propped in front of her like buttresses. She wore black aviator sunglasses to shield her failing eyes from the light, which gave her face all the openness of a vault. In old photographs, she looks most like a handicapped bomber pilot.

But with her three grandchildren, this woman was as gentle as a breeze. She loved us like nothing else in the world and we knew it. Whenever we came to visit, there were closetsful of wrapped presents, one for each day of the week; trips to town for new dresses with net petticoats and favorite desserts for dinner; baby chicks from the feed store and long afternoons on the porch swing in her arms. But her best gifts were her baths. When my night came she treated me like long lost royalty, filling the tub with suds and then beckoning me in, where she washed each of my limbs in turn and polished my skin with her great soft sponge. After she had dried me off I lay down for the next part of the ritual. First she anointed me with Jergen's Lotion, starting with my neck and finishing up with the soles of my feet. Then she reached for her dusting powder—Evening in Paris—and tickled me all over with the pale blue puff. When she had done, I knew I was precious. I was absolutely convinced I was loved, and nothing that has happened since, not even her death, has shaken that conviction.

So of course I recognized the fairy godmother in *The Princess and the Goblin* when I met her years later; she had bathed me, too. It was not until I was in seminary that I learned Macdonald was a Christian writer, and that what he had captured me with was a vision of the waters of baptism. When I was twelve, all I knew—both in that scene and in that Episcopal church—was that I stood in the presence of something holy, something that knew more about me than I knew about it. Worship offered me a way of staying with it, not of clarifying the mystery but of harnessing it, so that I was carried along in its numinous wake.

But this crystalline vision was not the only one I received in small-town Alabama. There were other varieties of religious experience loose in those parts, one of which sideswiped me in the person of a dark angel named Katybelle Prude. Katybelle cared for me and my sisters three days out of every week, cleaning house while we were at school and ironing clothes in the afternoons while we watched television. She was a strong black woman, trim and tightly packed, who padded around the house barefoot in her cotton skirts and colorful blouses. The most remarkable thing about her was the tin can she carried everywhere she went. Katybelle dipped snuff, and while she was discreet about it, there was no hiding the fact from three curious children who squealed and scattered whenever she spit into her can.

During the summers she had us full-time, which was sometimes more than she could stand, especially when it rained. One wet afternoon we all lined up in front of her ironing board, stupid with boredom, and watched her pound our clothes flat. The spit can leapt every time she brought the iron down. We watched it bounce with equal parts of hope and fear, ready to run the moment it took flight. Finally unable to bear our scrutiny any longer, Katybelle spoke.

"Y'all want to play?" she asked.

"Yes!" we declared in unison.

"You go get you some paper and pencils and we play," she said, so we did, and were back in no time with our crayons and magic markers, eager to be amused.

"First you draw you a yard with trees and flowers," she said, ironing in peace while we bent to her instructions. When we were through, she gave us the next step. "Now you draw you a pretty white house right in the middle of it, with a red chimney and little children playing in the yard," she said.

"Now what?" I said when I had finished.

"Now you put you a picket fence around that house to keep the dogs out," she said, "and don't forget the gate." Each of us did as she directed and were comparing our creations when Katybelle interrupted us.

"You think you through?" she said. "You girls ain't through. Now," she said, her eyes flashing and her voice coming from some place further down inside her tight body, "now you draw the whole sky on fire and that pretty white house going up in flames, because that how it gonna be when the end time come."

Katybelle knew something I did not know. That is what I decided on that rainy afternoon, clutching my drawing to my chest and running from the room. She had tricked me, but maybe she was right. Maybe God tricked people the same way, luring them with pretty pictures and then setting them on fire, to teach them a lesson about what was important and what was not. It was part of the same hard knowledge I had gained earlier in Ohio, the uneasy sense that God might be dangerous, a dazzling light that warmed but could also burn, reducing the whole world to ash.

I never was confirmed in the Episcopal Church. Race riots erupted at the state university; the rector got involved and church was not a safe place to be. My parents got involved as well and there was no safe place to be. Our Irish setter was poisoned, our bicycles were run over in the driveway of our house, and we were chased up trees by neighbor children with rocks. Before long we moved again, this time to Georgia, where I made Baptist friends whom I followed to church.

At sixteen, I was ready for what I heard there. The war in Vietnam was cranking up, an engine that threatened to devour boys my age in a very few years. People I knew were discovering sex and smoking marijuana. Life as I knew it was spinning out of control and I was looking for handles. I wanted to know what was right and what was wrong, how to live an honorable life and avoid trouble. I wanted to know how to get on God's good side and stay there, and the Baptist Church promised to tell me all these things. It was an offer I could not refuse. Under the influence of my red-headed best friend and her older brother, upon whom I had designs, I answered an altar call one summer's evening and was baptized by immersion soon afterward.

I was saved, but even before I could learn all the rules that would keep me saved, I ran afoul of them. Believing what the preacher said about how the church was a house of prayer for all people, I brought two hippies with me to that house one Wednesday night—runaways I had picked up hitchhiking on the road—and soon found myself banished along with them. It was a crushing revelation, but a revelation nonetheless. I knew, absolutely *knew* there was something to this Jesus-God business, and I knew with equal clarity that what I had just experienced was not it. Recognizing that I had been handed a counterfeit set me free to seek the real thing, and I never looked back.

My brief sojourn with the Baptists put me off institutional religion for a while, but when I was a sophomore in college two girls knocked on the door of my dormitory room one night and told me the Holy Spirit had sent them to find me. Because I could not think of a comparable reply, I let them in and endured their rehearsed spiel. When they had finished they both gazed at me expectantly, eager as spaniels for my reply. More out of courtesy than conviction, I bought what they were selling and knelt to accept Jesus Christ as my personal Lord and Savior. Then I sent them away and went for a walk to think about what I had just done, only it was hard to think or walk. My face felt flushed and hot; familiar scenery kept rippling before my eyes like a mirage on a hot road. When I lifted my feet to walk, they would not come all the way down. I limped back home with one foot on the sidewalk and the other in the air, while God just laughed and laughed.

I majored in religion because I liked the books and because the religion professors seemed more willing than anyone on campus to engage the moral and ethical issues of the day: the draft, the war, abortion. By the time I was a senior, my advisor had nudged me into applying for two different fellowships—one for doctoral work in religious studies and the other for a trial year in seminary. Had I received the first one, my career path would have been clear; I would have become a teacher. But I received the second one instead, and arrived at Yale Divinity School in the fall of 1973 without a clue what I was doing there.

The next three years were heady ones. I did well in classes that intrigued me, I made friends who became my family, and I found a church that became my home. It was the Episcopal Church—again—but this time I had words both for what I was seeking and what I found: liturgy, tradition, tolerance, transcendence, communion. Finding them all in one place, I once again experienced a call—not to belief, because that had already happened, and not to ordination, because that had not happened yet—but a call to belong to a particular body of believers and to join them in their sacramental faith.

I shared this call with the rector of the church during my second year in seminary, expecting him to welcome me at once, but instead he listened to my story and suggested that I wait a year. "Let's be sure you're really in love this time," he said, alluding to my numerous baptisms and conversions, and for the next year he directed both my reading and my prayers. I was confirmed when I was twenty-five years old, just weeks before my graduation from seminary.

I still had no intention of being ordained. In the first place, I could not imagine myself a "father," but another reason was that my theological education had made me wary of ordination. If the purpose of the church was to equip all God's people for ministry to the world—as I had been taught—then it made no sense to designate one of those people "the minister" in a congregation. Likewise, if that person's job was to support members of a congregation in their ministries to the world, it made no sense to set that person "apart" in ordination and then give that person an office inside the four safe walls of the church.

The whole arrangement seemed suspicious to me, and yet my own decision to become an Episcopalian had been shaped by the ordained ministry of one particular man, the rector who had so patiently led me to confirm my faith. His sermons were eloquent, his presence compelling, his theology imaginative, his ministry compassionate. He heard confessions at the back of the church on Saturdays; on Sundays he presided over a high mass that made holy mysteries as beautiful as they were nourishing. His interactions with me and a half dozen of my peers were so uncannily intuitive that we all latched on to him as our mentor and were all eventually ordained. His influence on each one of us was profound, but telling: the only way we could think of to be like him, to follow his example, was to become priests ourselves. Granted, we were all in seminary, but we were not all preparing for ordination. Several of us even switched denominations in order to make our emulation complete. I should add that he did nothing to encourage us, but for better or worse the exercise of his ordained ministry made us want to be ordained ministers too.

As one who had benefited from that ministry, I was aware both of its power and cost, and again I was wary of both. I spent enough time at the rectory to know how often the telephone rang, and how many times his supper was interrupted by someone knocking at the door. I knew how often people assumed he was available because he had no family and presumed to fill that gap for him. I knew how hard it was to get an appointment with him, and how little he was paid, but he endured all of that with grace and apparent good cheer. When I graduated, his present to me was Euell Gibbons' field guide, *Stalking the Wild Asparagus*. "So that you may feast in the wilderness," he wrote inside.

Over the next five years I struggled with the ordination question. I read books, prayed, made appointments with my bishop and canceled them. I entered diocesan programs and dropped out of them. I worked as a seminary administrator and a hospital chaplain. I took part-time jobs at churches. I moved a thousand miles away and back again in eight months. I listened for voices in the night and searched the sky for signs. If lasting preoccupation with the church constitutes a call, then I was called, but called to what? To be a priest, or to be a Christian? One midnight I asked God to tell me as plainly as possible what I was supposed to do.

"Anything that pleases you." That is the answer that came into my sleepy head.

"What?" I said, waking up. "What kind of an answer is that?"

"Do anything that pleases you," the voice in my head said again, "and belong to me."

That simplified things considerably. I could pump gas in Idaho or dig latrines in Pago Pago, as far as God was concerned, as long as I remembered whose I was. With no further distress, I decided that it would please me to become a priest, and to spend the rest of my life with a community willing to help me figure out what that meant. It did not strike me as an exalted idea at the time, nor does it seem so now, almost ten years later. The one true turning point in a person's life is when he or she joins the body of Christ, however that comes about—by sprinkling or by immersion, by proxy or by confession. That is the moment we join ranks with God. That is when we become the flesh and blood of God in the world. The decision to become ordained does not supersede that moment; it is simply one way of acting it out, one among very many others.

If my own experience can be trusted, then God does not call us once but many times. There are calls to faith and calls to ordination, but in between there are calls to particular communities and calls to particular tasks within them—calls into and out of relationships as well as calls to seek God wherever God may be found. Sometimes those calls ring clear as bells and sometimes they are barely audible, but in any case we are not meant to hear them all by ourselves. It was part of God's genius to incorporate us as one body, so that our ears have other ears, other eyes, minds, hearts, and voices to help us interpret what we have heard. Together we can hear our calls, and together we can answer them, if only we will listen for the still, small voice that continues to speak to us in the language of our lives.

CHAPTER THREE

Vocation

Not too long ago I spoke with a recent college graduate about his desire to be ordained. He was an articulate Christian who had been active in campus ministry and deeply influenced by the Episcopal chaplain at his school. He was bright, committed, and knowledgeable about the faith, but as he talked I grew perplexed. He did not want to serve a church, did not think he would like being held accountable by a denominational body, and was not attracted to a ministry of the sacraments, although he did believe he would like to preach once a month or so.

"Then why do you want to be ordained?" I asked him. He thought a while and finally said, "For the identity, I guess. So I could sit down next to someone on a bus who looked troubled and ask them how they were without them thinking I'm trying to hustle them. So I could walk up to someone on the street and do the same thing. So I could be up front about what I believe, in public as well as in private. So I would have the credentials to be the kind of Christian I want to be." His honesty was both disarming and disheartening. God help the church if clergy are the only Christians with "credentials," and God help all those troubled people on the bus if they have to wait for an ordained person to come along before anyone speaks to them.

When God calls, people respond in a variety of ways. Some pursue ordination and others put pillows over their heads, but the vast majority seek to answer God by changing how they live their more or less ordinary lives. It can be a frustrating experience, because deciding what is called for means nothing less than deciding what it means to be a Christian in a post-Christian world. Is it a matter of changing who you are—becoming a kinder, more spiritual person? Or is it a matter of changing what you do—looking for a new job, becoming more involved at church, or witnessing to the neighbors? What does God want from us, and how can we comply?

In many ways, those who pursue ordination take the easy way out. They choose a prescribed role that seems to meet all the requirements, and take up full-time residence in the church. They forego the hard work of straddling two different worlds, while those they serve have no such luxury. Those in the pulpit may know where they belong, but the people in the pews hold dual citizenship. When they come together as the church, that is where they belong—in God's country, which is governed by love. But when they leave that place, they cross the border into another country governed by other, less forgiving laws—and they live there too.

One man I know describes his dilemma this way. "On Sunday morning," he says, "I walk into a world that is the way God meant it to be. People are considerate of one another. Strangers are welcomed. We pray for justice and peace. Our sins are forgiven. We all face in one direction, and we worship the same God. When it's over, I get in my car to drive home feeling so full of love it's unbelievable, but by the time I've gone twenty minutes down the road it has already begun to wear off. By Monday morning it's all gone, and I've got another whole week to wait until Sunday rolls around again."

It is not a new problem he describes. From the very beginning, being a Christian has meant being a sojourner in a strange land. The reversal in our own day is that for many people it is the church, and not the rest of the world, that is strange. As the moat between the two has widened, the old bridges have become obsolete, leaving commuters to paddle across by themselves as best they can.

What many Christians are missing in their lives is a sense of vocation. The word itself means a call or summons, so that having a vocation means more than having a job. It means answering a specific call; it means doing what one is meant to do. In religious language, it means participating in the work of God, something that few lay people believe they do. Immersed in the corporate worlds of business and finance, and in the domestic worlds of household and family, it is hard for them to see how their lives have anything to do with the life of God. From time to time they pay visits to their priests, confessing how they ache for more meaningful work. Lay people are doing their jobs, but are they doing the jobs they were born to do?

Somewhere along the way we have misplaced the ancient vision of the church as a priestly people—set apart for ministry in baptism, confirmed and strengthened in worship, made manifest in service to the world. That vision is a foreign one to many church members, who have learned from colloquial usage that "minister" means the ordained person in a congregation, while "lay person" means someone who does not engage in full-time ministry. Professionally speaking that is fair enough—ordained people make their livings in ministry, and lay people do not—but speaking ecclesiastically, it is a disaster. Language like that turns clergy into purveyors of religion and lay people into consumers, who shop around for the church that offers them the best product.

But affirming the ministry of every baptized Christian is not an idea that appeals to many lay people these days. It sounds like more work, and most of them have all the work they can do. It sounds like more responsibility, while most of them are staggering under loads that are already too heavy. I will never forget the woman who listened to my speech on the ministry of the laity as God's best hope for the world and said, "I'm sorry, but I don't want to be that important."

Like many of those who sit beside her at church, she hears the invitation to ministry as an invitation to *do* more—to lead the every member canvass, or cook supper for the homeless, or teach vacation church school. Or she hears the invitation to ministry as an invitation to *be* more—to be more generous, more loving, more religious. No one has ever introduced her to the idea that her ministry might involve being just who she already is and doing just what she already does, with one difference: namely, that she understand herself to be God's person in and for the world.

However simple it sounds, I suppose that invitation will always frighten people, if only because they have heard such hair-raising tales about what happens to God's representatives. Whether they are reading the Bible or the newspaper, the bottom line is the same: God's people draw fire. Meanwhile, however, their fear causes them to surrender their power, and what they are willing to lay down, someone else is always willing to pick up. Traditionally, it is the clergy who have filled that role, keeping the church neat by gathering up all the power the laity have dropped there. Part of it is their genuine if misguided desire to be helpful, but the rest of it is megalomania—their perverse notion that they are the only ones who can be trusted with the ministry of the church.

Almost five hundred years ago, a German monk named Martin Luther wrestled the same problem. In his day, clergy ruled the church like princes, selling salvation and getting fat off alms. They got away with it because they claimed a special relationship with God. They asserted the superiority of their own vocations and elected themselves to the highest offices of the church, until all that was left for the laity was to attend Mass as they might attend the theater, watching mutely as the clergy consumed communion all by themselves, and paying their dues on the way out.

In his address to the German nobles, Luther attacked this farce. He made careful distinction between a Christian's vocation and a Christian's office, suggesting that our offices are what we do for a living—teacher, shopkeeper, homemaker, priest—and that none of them is any dearer to the heart of God than another. In our offices we exercise the diversity of our gifts, playing our parts in the ongoing life of the world. Our offices are the "texts" of our lives, to use a dramatic term, but the "subtext" is the common vocation to which we are all called at baptism. Whatever our individual offices in the world, our mutual vocation is to serve God through them.

> Only look at your tools, your needle, your thimble, your beer barrel, your articles of trade, your scales, your measures, and you will find this saying written on them. You will not be able to look anywhere where it does not strike your eyes. None of the things with which you deal daily are too trifling to tell you this incessantly, if you are but willing to hear it; and there is no lack of such preaching, for you have as many preachers as there are transactions, commodities, tools and other implements in your house and estate, and they shout this to your face: "My dear, use me toward your neighbor as you would want him to act toward you with that which is his."[1]

My office, then, is in the church. That is where I do what I do, and what I do makes me different from those among whom I serve. But my *vocation* is to be God's person in the world, and that makes me the same as those among whom I serve. What we have in common is our baptism, that turning point in each one of our lives when we were received into the household of God and charged to confess the faith of Christ crucified, proclaim his resurrection, and share in his eternal priesthood. That last phrase is crucial. Our baptisms are our ordinations, the moments at which we are set apart as God's people to share Christ's ministry, whether or not we ever wear clerical collars around our necks. The instant we rise dripping from the waters of baptism and the sign of the cross is made upon our foreheads, we are marked as Christ's own forever.

I have often wondered whether the church would be even smaller than it is if that cross were made not with water but with permanent ink—a nice deep purple, perhaps—so that all who bore Christ's mark bore it openly, visibly, for the rest of their lives. In many ways, I think, that is the chief difference between the ministry of the baptized and the ministry of the ordained. The ordained consent to be visible in a way that the baptized do not. They agree to let people look at them as they struggle with their own baptismal vows: to continue in the apostles' teaching and fellowship, to resist evil, to proclaim the good news of God in Christ, to seek and serve Christ in all persons, to strive for justice and peace among all people. Those are not the vows of the ordained, but the baptized, even though we do not seem to know how to honor them in the course of ordinary life on earth.

Perhaps we should revive Luther's vision of the priesthood of all believers, who are ordained by God at baptism to share Christ's ministry in the world—a body of people united by that one common vocation, which they pursue across the gamut of their offices in the world. It is a vision that requires a rich and disciplined imagination, because it is largely a matter of learning to see in a different way. To believe in one's own priesthood is to see the extraordinary dimensions of an ordinary life, to see the hand of God at work in the world and to see one's own hands as necessary to that work. Whether those hands are diapering an infant, assembling an automobile or balancing a corporate account, they are God's hands, claimed by God at baptism for the accomplishment of God's will on earth. There are plenty who will decline the honor, finding it either too fearsome or too intrusive to be taken seriously, but those willing to accept the challenge will want to know more about what a priest does, exactly.

The first thing to say is that a priest is a representative person—a *parson*—who walks the shifting boundary between heaven and earth, representing God to humankind, representing humankind to God, and serving each in the other's name. It is not possible to exercise such priesthood without participating in Christ's own, which means there are no entrepreneurs in ministry, only partners. Pursuing that vocation, priests are likely to wear a hundred different hats—social worker, chauffeur, cook, financial advisor, community organizer, babysitter, philanthropist, marriage counselor, cheerleader, friend—but whatever hat they happen to be wearing at the time, priests remember that they wear it as God's person, for God's sake, in God's name.

Everything else a priest does comes to focus in worship, where all of God's ministers—the baptized ones and the ordained ones—approach God through the sacraments of word and table. In the early church, believers decided it was not practical for all of them to preside over community worship, so they elected different members of the body to officiate from week to week. Sometimes they drew lots, making it clear that the job had nothing to do with superiority. It was a representative function, whereby one member of the congregation stepped forward to do what everyone present was able to do. That person's ministry did not overshadow theirs, but affirmed it, so that what they did together in worship became a model for what they did after worship as they returned to their offices in the world.

In our own time, the lots are fixed. Through long and sometimes arduous processes, we choose certain people to lead us in worship, so that we become accustomed to hearing them from the pulpit and seeing them at the altar—so accustomed that it is easy to forget they are not the only ministers in the church. The ministry of the ordained is no substitute for the ministry of the baptized; it is a prototype, copied from Christ's own, that offers the whole people of God a pattern for seeking and responding to the Lord's presence in our midst.

While preaching and celebrating sacraments are discrete tasks, the two particular functions to which I was ordained, they are also metaphors for the whole church's understanding of life and faith. For me, to preach is first of all to immerse myself in the word of God, to look inside every sentence and underneath every phrase for the layers of meaning that have accumulated there over the centuries. It is to examine my own life and the life of the congregation with the same care, hunting the connections between the word on the page and the word at work in the world. It is to find my own words for bringing those connections to life, so that others can experience them for themselves. When that happens—when the act of preaching becomes a source of revelation for me as well as for those who listen to me—then the good news every sermon proclaims is that the God who acted is the God who acts, and that the Holy Spirit is alive and well in the world.

Understood in this way, preaching becomes something the whole community participates in, not only through their response to a particular sermon but also through identifying with the preacher. As they listen week after week, they are invited to see the world the way the preacher does—as the realm of God's activity—and to make connections between their Christian faith and their lives the same way they hear them made from the pulpit. If the preaching they hear is effective, it will not hand them sacks of wisdom and advice to take home and consume during the week, but invite them into the field to harvest those fruits for themselves, until they become preachers in their own right. Preaching is not something an ordained minister does for fifteen minutes on Sundays, but what the whole congregation does all week long; it is a way of approaching the world, and of gleaning God's presence there.

Likewise, the sacraments of the church embody a broad Christian understanding of life on earth: chiefly, that the most ordinary things in the world are signs of grace. The God who created them and called them good keeps on doing so. Through the sacraments, we are invited to understand that all the things of this world are good enough to bear the presence of God and to deepen the relationship between heaven and earth. To glimpse the holiness of ordinary bread or wine or oil or water is to begin to suspect that holiness may be hiding in other things as well. Holiness may be lurking inside a green leaf, a clay cup, a clean sheet, a freshly sawn board; it may be just below the surface of a key, a clock, a shiny stone. To draw a line around the seven sacraments for which the church has rites is to underestimate the grace of God and the holiness of the creation. According to the catechism, "God does not limit himself to these rites; they are patterns of countless ways by which God uses material things to reach out to us."

Sacraments not only hallow the stuff of the world; they also hallow our handling of that stuff. They give us something to look at, something to taste and smell, something to feel upon our skin and experience for ourselves. They give us something to do with our hands and with our bodies as well—walking up to receive communion, bending over the baptismal font, kneeling so that hands may be laid upon our heads. We may spend our whole lives learning what those sacraments mean, but the experience of them exceeds our understanding of them. Reaching out to handle God, it is we who are handled, gently but with powerful effect.

Several weeks ago I took communion to an elderly and beloved woman at her home. She sat heaped in her wheelchair as I turned the television tray between us into an altar: tiny chalice, tiny paten, and a yellow rose from the garden, all spread on an embossed white paper napkin. Because she was ninety-seven years old and all but blind, I suggested that she not bother with a prayer book. "I'll read all the lines," I said, "yours and mine too. You just join in on the parts you know." She nodded and we began, each of us delivering our lines on cue until I came to the Great Thanksgiving. Then, when I raised my hands, she raised hers too, the sleeves of her flowered gown falling down her bony arms as she lifted her gnarled fists into the air. We faced each other across the table, mirror images of one another.

"Holy and gracious Father," I began, "in your infinite love you made us for yourself...."

"In your infinite love," she said slowly, tasting each word.

"And, when we had fallen into sin and become subject to evil and death," I went on, "you, in your mercy, sent Jesus Christ...."

"In your mercy," she said, smiling as though someone she knew had just entered the room. When I realized she meant to say the whole prayer with me, I waited for her to catch up and we prayed it together, our voices looping through one another in an unstudied duet. I had thought they were my lines, but they turned out to be hers as well. No one had fooled her, all those years she sat watching someone else bless the bread and the wine. She knew she was a priest.

The ministries of word and sacrament may begin in church, but they never end there. They are borne into the world by all baptized Christians, who exercise them in more ways and places than the ordained alone ever could. How, exactly, do they do that in a world that is indifferent if not hostile to their ministrations? Well, in the first place, it is best not to be too formal about these things. By the ministry of the word, I don't mean preaching on the steps of the public library or witnessing door to door. I mean engaging in the discipline of reading and studying and arguing with and wondering about and meditating on and living with the word of God in Scripture. I mean letting its stories and images come to life so that they become daily points of reference and sources of unceasing insight. I mean understanding the Bible as an anthology of God's relationship with our ancestors and as an invitation to seek a relationship of our own. I mean believing in Scripture as evidence of God's power to change lives and as a hot coal that may ignite our own lives even now.

These are all the disciplines of a preacher, whose job it is to interpret the good news of the past so that it is understood as the good news of the present and future. While a lay person's trips to the pulpit may be few, this good news cannot help but creep into everyday discourse, until conversations with colleagues, midnight talks with children, and telephone calls to ailing friends all resound with the faith, hope, and love of someone engaged in the ministry of the word.

Whether the minister is a baptized one or an ordained one, the sacrament of the word calls for a light touch. The worst sermons in the world are those that treat Scripture like a mold that life must be pressed into, using a bit of reality here, a scrap of experience there in order to "illustrate" the truth of God's word. What they forget is that Scripture was first put into our hands not as a *prescription* for life but as a *description* of it, full of wisdom intended to serve us in our living of it. Consequently, the best sermons are those that begin with life, telling stories that have the ring of truth and suggesting the ways in which God's word addresses the often perplexing truths of our lives.

The ministry of the sacraments involves an equally light touch. On Sundays, some of us watch others of us handle holy bread and wine at altars carved with the symbols of our faith. What we see are outward and visible signs of an inward and spiritual grace, but we also remember that God is not limited to the seven rites we have written for our corporate worship. God reaches out to us in countless ways through the material things of our lives: there are altars everywhere with sacraments just waiting to be discovered and celebrated. Anyone who has made annual pilgrimages home for Thanksgiving knows that the dining room table is one such altar, where sacraments of turkey and sweet potato pie evince the grace of a family whose loving of one another may from time to time far exceed their liking.

A gardener's altar may be his garden, where sacraments of seed and bud contain the grace of God's life-giving power; a painter's altar may be her easel, where sacraments of canvas and oil evoke the grace of God's creative genius; a father's altar may be his lap, where sacraments of children exhibit the grace of God's love. Such everyday sacraments may be easier to discern in our personal lives—sacraments of friends, family, home, nature—but since we are called to be priests wherever we are, it is important that we learn to recognize them in our professional lives as well. Wherever our *offices* are, that is where we are called to exercise our *vocation* as ministers of word and sacrament.

A physician's altar may be her examining room, where sacraments of other people's bodies remind her of her kinship with all creation. A word processor's altar may be his desk, where sacraments of software and computer printouts mark his participation in the human effort to communicate. A truck driver's altar may be the cab of his truck, where the sacrament of his citizen's band radio connects him to other human beings who do not wish to be lonely. The search for sacraments becomes a search for our connections to God and to one another, and there is no end to them. They may sometimes be difficult to recognize in all the cares and occupations of our lives, and they may sometimes reveal truths we would rather not see, but to deny their existence—to declare any part of our lives devoid of sacraments—is to deny the sovereignty of God.

Those who are ordained tend to exercise the ministries of word and sacrament in established patterns because it is their office to do so, but they need watching. Because their spheres are limited, they tend to forget that God's activity is not. They may imply that people must come to the church for their sacraments, as if they were their property, to be loaned as they see fit. They may infer that God is more comfortable with polished brass and stained glass than with the gaudy disarray of the world.

Take the eucharist, for instance. On Wednesdays at noon, I celebrate Holy Communion for the five or six souls who have found their ways to a chapel hidden deep in the garden of a downtown church. It is a brief, quiet service that nourishes all of us who participate. But just lately I have been daydreaming about moving the celebration to the front steps of the church, thirty feet from one of the busiest intersections in the city. The fantasy is compelling: sweeping the trash off the steps, picking the newspapers and brown-bagged vodka bottles out of the bushes, and setting up an altar underneath the telephone and power lines—smoothing out the altar cloth as someone asks for directions and setting the table as someone else asks for a quarter—celebrating with my back against the front doors of the church and my face toward the rapid transit terminal, the bank, the fire station, the street—giving thanks on behalf of all the pedestrians walking by, all the cars, buses, trucks, and ambulances competing for headway, honking their horns. It is not something I will do, but I wonder why not.

Our worship tells us the household of God was not meant to stay in the house. The gospel we hear proclaimed week after week is God's good news about the redemption of the world, in which we are invited to take part. Our prayers are prayers for the church and for the *world*. We confess our sins against God and our neighbors, and we do not mean just those sitting beside us in our pews. The two great sacraments of the church remind us that we are *sent*: "Send them into the world in witness to your love," we pray for those about to be baptized. "Send us now into the world in peace," we pray for ourselves in the communion service. Even the relatively exclusive sacrament of marriage includes a prayer that God make the couple's life together "a sign of Christ's love to this sinful and broken world." There is simply no getting around it. If the church is where we learn who and whose we are, the world is where we are called to put that knowledge to use.

Answering that call requires no particular virtues. Those who have been marked as Christ's own forever have everything they need, but a good imagination helps. There is even a chance that the Christian vocation is above all a vocation to imagine—to see what God sees when God looks at the world, and to believe that God's dreams can come true.

NOTES
1. Gustaf Wingren, *Luther on Vocation* (Philadelphia: Fortress Press, 1957), 72.

CHAPTER FOUR

Imagination

A friend of mine clearly remembers the summer he lost his imagination. He was eleven years old, a distracted fifth grader who yearned for the last day of school so that he could return full time to the fields of play. Memories of the previous summer spurred him on, long days spent lying on his belly in the backyard, racing miniature cars and trucks with his friends. When the last bell of the school year rang, he ran home to get everything ready, and next morning he hauled it all outside. With the early sun heating up behind his back, he sat down in his special place surrounded by special toys and waited for the delicious feeling to creep over him, but nothing happened. He picked up his favorite truck and ran its wheels over the ground. "Rrrrrr!" he roared, as he had done so many times before, but it was not the sound of an engine this time. It was the sound of a boy's voice pretending to be an engine, and he was suddenly self-conscious. One by one he tried all his old tricks, but none of them worked. The bridge to his old world was gone. He no longer had access to it, and the loss opened up a hollow place inside of him. He looked at his toys and saw what he had never seen before: they were small and cheap, a child's toys. It had all been a silly game. Standing up, he dusted himself off and left the fossils of his dream time lying in the yard.

Everyone has some memory like this, a moment when the magic failed and nothing was ever the same again. In that moment, a world that had been plump with meaning became flat and one-dimensional. All the old doors into it disappeared, their cracks and keyholes sealing over to become one impenetrable wall. It is not only an individual experience but an evolutionary one as well. Stroll through any museum of human history and watch the tableaux change, from large children in animal skins painting figures on the walls of their caves to men in beaver top hats standing in front of locomotives and skyscrapers. As our ability to control the world around us has increased, our respect for its mystery has decreased. Our chief interest in anything—a tree, another person, God—is its usefulness to us and not its existence in and of itself. We have forgotten how to submit ourselves to life on earth. We have become the worst kind of consumers, devouring the creation whole and spitting out the seeds.

The church's central task is an imaginative one. By that I do not mean a fanciful or fictional task, but one in which the human capacity to imagine—to form mental pictures of the self, the neighbor, the world, the future, to envision new realities—is both engaged and transformed. Everyone is born with imagination. Small children are virtuosi, perhaps because their fresh minds are not yet hedged by the constraints of "reality." They look at stars and see pinholes punched in the dark cloth that separates them from everlasting brightness. They drape towels over their shoulders and become monarchs in ermine cloaks with toilet brush scepters. They create whole civilizations in the exposed roots of an old oak tree, complete with twig fences, acorn currency, and lakes made from jar lids full of tap water.

Part of their secret is their natural ability to employ all their senses. Small children have not yet learned to view the world around them as scenery, a flat backdrop to walk past on their way to somewhere else. They are still immersed in it, up to their eyes in colors, up to their ears in sounds, with fingertips that ache to stroke a sparrow and noses that can find a creek in the dark by its smell. They live in a world where sharp distinctions need not be made, where green is a texture as well as a hue, where rain has a taste as important as its temperature, where the sound of sunlight can be deafening at noon. It is a world that includes dangers and great sadnesses—hornets' nests and wounded animals with pleading eyes—but even those are vivid and full of meaning, more proof of a world that pushes back when it is pressed against. Having given themselves to the experience of such a world, children do not seem to have learned the sad trick of removing themselves from it again. Their imagination thrives on the sensual details that their elders have learned to take for granted.

Their other advantage is their ignorance of adult notions of what things are supposed to be and do. Adults may agree that a comb is for combing hair, but children are not so limited. They know that a comb is also a musical instrument, a sifter for seashells hidden in the sand, a back scratcher for dogs, and a tool for making racetracks for ants. Adults know that money is for spending, but children have different values. They prefer cents to dollars, and they like to hang on to them. How many they have is more important to them than what they are worth, and what they might buy with them is far less interesting than the music they make, or the faces on them, or the way they reflect the light in a glass of water.

To apprentice oneself to a child is to learn that the world is full of wonders, a world in which nothing is simply what it seems because everything is packed with endless possibilities of usefulness and meaning. To enter that world, all you have to do is surrender your certainty that you already know what everything is and is for; all you have to do is start over again, assuming nothing and learning to approach every created thing with awe.

It is a process of conversion—or reconversion—a recovery of what we once knew and forgot. Why we forget remains a puzzle. Do we lose our imaginations to our schooling? Stars are not holes punched in the sky; they are astral bodies revolving in space. Or do we lose our imaginations to our growing mastery of the world? Our dream image of a chariot with six white horses fades as an actual red bicycle with streamers on the handlebars comes into focus. Or is losing our imaginations part of a natural process, like shedding baby teeth?

Wittingly or unwittingly, we human beings are driven by our images of ourselves, of other people, of God and the world—images that come to us both from within and without. Some images rise straight from the unconscious, swimming out of its deep waters to present themselves to us in dreams and meditations. Many others are pressed upon us from the outside, first by parents and then by all the shapers of our vision: teachers, preachers, authors, artists, newscasters, movie makers, advertisers, and television scriptwriters—all of them presenting us with pictures of the world and our place in it, none of them agreeing about who we are, exactly, or what we are supposed to be doing here.

Some tell us the world is a wonderful and romantic place we should hasten to explore, while others warn us of a violent planet, laced with poison and threat. Some want us to believe that what we own will make us happy, or how we look, while others encourage us to invest in the happiness of others. Some advise us to give up on a God who never was and save ourselves instead, while others describe their encounters with beings of light who lead them through other dimensions of time and space. Choosing whom to believe, we choose the images that shape our lives, and the competition for our allegiance is fierce.

Meanwhile the Christian tradition has its own set of images, and while they are not free from corruption or contradiction (Did Christ come to bring peace or a sword? Is God a hanging judge or a forgiving father?), still they offer us a particular perspective on our lives that is different from those offered us by Madison Avenue, Wall Street, or Hollywood. Both our Scripture and our liturgy are full of images that mean to tell us who we are—images of Eden, Exodus, and Easter—images of water, bread, and wine—images with power to change lives, but only for those who choose them.

For the world beyond the church they carry no such power. That world is inspired by different images—images of wealth and dominance, self-sufficiency and physical perfection—that are as slick as magazine ads and as hypnotic as television commercials. Because we are members of the world as well as the church, we know how compelling they are. They appeal to our deepest hungers: the hunger to be safe, to be happy, to be loved. They appeal to the same part of us that holy images do, and in many ways the ongoing struggle of faith is the struggle to choose between those that have power to save us and those that do not.

"Faith," says theologian James Whitehead, "is the enduring ability to imagine life in a certain way."[1] If he is right, then the human capacity for imagination is one the church cannot afford to ignore. While it may seem more respectable to approach faith as an intellectual exercise or more satisfying to approach it as an emotional one, our relationship to God is not simply a matter of what we think or how we feel. It is more comprehensive than that, and more profound. It is a full-bodied relationship in which mind and heart, spirit and flesh, are converted to a new way of experiencing and responding to the world. It is the surrender of one set of images and the acceptance of another. It is a matter of learning to see the world, each other, and ourselves as God sees us, and to live as if God's reality were the only one that mattered.

But to suggest that conversion is an imaginative act is to risk not being taken seriously, because imagination has a bad reputation among people of faith. In the first place, it is a synonym for fantasy. "It is only your imagination," we tell children afraid of dragons in the dark, aiming to convince them that the reality in front of their eyes is more real than the reality behind them. It may be a good move as far as their mental health is concerned, but it is also a lesson about the nature of imagination. The child who listens learns that imagination does not deal in truth but in illusion; she learns her imagination is not to be trusted.

What, then, do you tell that same child when she begins to ask what God looks like or where heaven can be found? Can she find the answers to those questions in the reality that lies in front of her eyes? Or is it time to go behind them again, into the world of her imagination, where a different reality prevails? If she does, she will always wonder whether what she finds there is truth or illusion. It goes with the territory, territory that the Bible has posted.

"The imagination of man's heart is evil from his youth," God decides in the eighth chapter of Genesis. While the New Revised Standard Version substitutes "inclination" for "imagination," which may be nearer the truth, the English-speaking church has lived with the older translation for hundreds of years, linking the human ability to imagine with the human ability to do evil. By this token, human imagination persuaded Adam and Eve to order apples for breakfast; human imagination built the tower of Babel. Most dangerous of all, human imagination played God. Everyone knew what God had done, breathing on a pile of dust and turning out a human being. In a parody of creation, human beings followed suit, heating a pile of gold and turning out a god, a small golden calf to worship and control. Their idolatrous creativity was their undoing. "You shall not make for yourself a graven image, or any likeness of anything that is in heaven above, or that is in the earth beneath, or that is in the water under the earth; you shall not bow down to them or serve them," God instructed Moses to tell the rest of us (Exodus 20:4 RSV). Henceforth, the making of images was against the law, not because they were wicked in themselves but because we became so charmed by our own creations that we imagined them superior to God's. The warning was not to imagine ourselves God's equals, nor to pit our images against God's own.

While this ancient legacy lies all but forgotten in the trunks of time, we are still ambivalent about the role of imagination in the life of faith. Is an imagined thing a true thing or a false thing? Is it real or not? What good is it, if it cannot be proved? And what about objective truth? Are we really prepared to confess that God is the property of our imaginations?

No. But we may be prepared to confess that our imaginations are the property of God. All our other faculties are useless to us; we cannot perceive God as we would a ginkgo tree or a speckled trout or children chasing a yellow dog. Those clues to God's existence are all available to our senses, but the One whom they suggest is not. The reality in front of our eyes is not deep enough to contain its creator. When we sense God's presence, we glimpse another reality, one that we may enter only by the door of our imaginations.

By imagination, I mean first of all the human ability to form a mental image of something not present to the senses. Anyone who reads does this all the time. Black marks on a white page are interpreted by the eye as words, which communicate particular meanings to the mind, where images are formed. If the images are strong ones, surprising things can happen. Black marks on a white page can produce tears, or sweat, or laughter. A while back I read James Michener's *Hawaii*, with its harrowing description of a sailing ship's repeated failure to navigate the stormy Strait of Magellan. The missionaries on board were lashed to their bunks as the ship heaved back and forth; waves crashed over the deck, washing food supplies overboard and pickling every surface with salt. This went on for weeks, until everyone was sick with scurvy or dying of thirst. Safe in my own chair and two hundred miles from the nearest ocean, I became as seasick as anyone on board.

Such is the power of the imagination, not only to make pictures in the mind but to make them so real they evoke physical response in the one who imagines them. The distinction between inner and outer reality becomes blurred. What I see behind my eyes changes what I see in front of them; my imagination shapes my perception so that I must look not once but twice at the world to see it whole.

Walking down the street, I see a wild-looking character sitting on the steps of the library. His gray hair is matted. His dense beard covers the slogan on his grimy T-shirt. His small darting eyes are as volatile as a hawk's. I look once and think "drifter." I look twice and think "John the Baptist," and in that imaginative act my relationship to the man is changed.

Reading the newspaper, I see a map of the world with symbols denoting war, earthquake, famine. There are black lines separating this country from that, this people from that. I note with some relief that the area in which I live is free of symbols. I look once and think, "Thank God I'm an American." I look twice and think, "God help me, I'm an earthling," and in that imaginative act my relationship to the world in which I live is changed.

I am writing a sermon on Saint Luke. I know he was a physician and I know he was an evangelist, but everyone knows that and it is boring. I start imagining his black bag, his doctor's bag, and what is in it. I look once and see pills and bandages; I look twice and discover it is full of gospel stories with power to heal, and in that imaginative act a sermon on gospel medicine begins.

The theological word for this experience is *revelation*, but the process, I believe, is imagination. In the imaginative act, two ideas are struck together and sparks leap through the air between them, revealing familiar notions in a new light. There are Native Americans who call this "looking twice" at the world. First, they say, we must "bring our eyes together in front" so that we notice every drop of dew in the grass, the steam rising from damp anthills in the sunshine. Then we must look again, directing our gaze at "the very edge of what is visible" so that we see visions, cloud people, animals that hurry past us in the dark. "You must learn to look at the world twice if you wish to see all there is to see," writes Jamake Hightower, a Blackfoot Indian.[2]

It is not a new idea. "Consider the lilies of the field, how they grow," Jesus said long before, inviting his disciples to the same kind of vision. "Look at the fig tree, and all the trees." Look at seeds, weeds, coins, sheep, nets, pearls, birds; look at parents and children, stewards and laborers, farmers and fishermen; look at women sweeping and baking bread.

45

"The kingdom of heaven is like yeast that a woman took and mixed in with three measures of flour," Jesus taught, reminding us that the kingdom is to be found in the most ordinary details of our ordinary lives. It may be hidden, but it is there, if we will look not once but twice.

In the imaginative act, we are grasped whole. Revelation is not a matter of thinking or feeling, intuiting or sensing, working from the left side of the brain or the right. It is a shocking gift of new sight that obliterates such distinctions, grabbing us by our lapels and turning us around, so that when we are set back down again we see everything from a new angle. We reason differently, feel differently, act differently. Imagination does more than affect us; it effects change in our lives. Physicians use guided imagery to heal their patients; coaches teach it to their athletes. Elementary school teachers have begun asking their young students to close their eyes and imagine large, colorful numbers in the air: a yellow two plus a red three equaling a big orange five. It is play, but it works. When the children open their eyes and pick up their pencils, their sums add up. Over and over again, the human imagination turns out to be the place where vision is formed and reformed, where human beings encounter an inner reality with power to transform the other realities of their lives.

In recent years the church has begun to get in on the act, however timidly. Devotional books offer imaginative exercises for use in prayer and the reading of Scripture; preaching texts stress the importance of imagery in the sermon. A few denominations even set aside quiet time during worship for congregational meditation. But on the whole, we remain skittish about exposing our faith to our imaginations.

During my tenure as a coordinator of Christian education, I heard a lot from people about their hunger to know the Bible, so I hired professors from a nearby seminary and offered regular courses on the Old and New Testaments. People told me the descriptions sounded like just what they needed, but that was usually the last I saw of them. The classes were small and sporadically attended, while classes on religion and the arts or parenting techniques overflowed their banks. Yet every quarter, people asked for more Bible courses. They said they wanted more; they were not getting enough. So I offered more Bible and still no one came.

Finally I got the message. "Bible" was a code word for "God." People were not hungry for information about the Bible; they were hungry for an experience of God, which the Bible seemed to offer them. So I laid off the seminary professors and offered a class on biblical meditation instead, which filled up at once. The plan was simple: every week we locked the door, took off our shoes and closed our eyes while we listened to a story about the raising of Lazarus, or the feeding of the five thousand, or John's vision of the heavenly Jerusalem. We shut down the reality in front of our eyes. We hung "Gone fishing" signs on our eyelids and let our imaginations take us places we had never been.

We were scared witless by Lazarus stumbling mummy-blind from his tomb. We handled the precious stones that encrusted the walls of Jerusalem; we dangled our feet in the river of life that ran through the middle of it. We dug our hands into baskets of dried fish and bread, eating from them until our belts cut off our circulation. Afterward we compared notes on where we had been and what we had seen, finding out that most of us had gone on the same trip, although we remembered different things about it.

The week we listened to Matthew's story about Peter's botched walk across the water, most of us got soaked. One woman was overcome by the stench of fish scales in the bottom of the boat, while another amazed herself by taking off her shirt. "All the other disciples had taken theirs off to row," she insisted, "so I just took mine off and rowed too." One man found that he simply could not make himself step on to the water. "I could not do it," he confessed. "Every time I tried, my knees turned to rubber. But Jesus forgave me. When I told him I could not do it, he said it was all right. And you know what? I believed him."

With very few exceptions, participants in the class discovered a visceral connection with Scripture they had never known before. Through their imaginations, they understood things about themselves and the other people in their lives and about God that they said they would never forget, but they remained reluctant to claim their revelations. "I have to keep reminding myself that I just made it up," one person said. "It was like I was there, or Jesus was here, but I know it didn't really happen."

Even more plaintive were those who could not complete the meditations for fear of getting them wrong. "What if I imagine Jesus tall and he was short?" one class member worried out loud. "Or what if I imagine him laughing and he was really mad? The way it's written down is the way it happened. Who am I to mess with that?" It is the question everyone who reckons with Scripture must finally ask, and it is a good one: what is real and what is not? What is really in the text and what is my own wishful thinking?

I want to address that question at length in the next chapter, but meanwhile there is a point to be made about honoring the faithful imagination. Imagination is no pedant, presenting systematic theologies for our edification. It has no point to make, no ax to grind. It is more like a child roaming the neighborhood on a free afternoon, following first the smell of fresh bread in an oven, then the glint of something bright in the grass—led by curiosity, by hunger, by hope, to explore the given world from its highest branches to its deepest roots because it is wonderful and terrible and because it is there.

When imagination comes home and empties its pockets, of course there will be some sorting to do. Keep the cat's-eye marble, the Japanese beetle wing, the red feather, the penny. Jettison the bottle cap, the broken glass, the melted chocolate stuck with lint. But do not scold imagination for bringing it all home, or for collecting it in the first place. There are no treasures without some trash, and the Holy Spirit can be trusted to go with us when we wander and to lead us back home again, with eyes far wiser for all they have seen.

When I was young, my mother entertained me on rainy afternoons by giving me a book full of word and picture games: crossword puzzles, connect-the-dots, fill-in-the-blanks. Those were all fine, but none of them was my favorite. My favorite was the page that held a perfectly ordinary drawing—a tree, perhaps, or a playroom—in which other figures were cleverly hidden. "How Many Animals Can You Find In This Picture?" the caption read, and I would stare and stare, turning the page around and around, until I had discovered them all: giraffes, lions, elephants, zebras, hippos, and baboons.

It was for me a source of unending delight—to find the hidden figures, to confront the ordinary in full confidence that it would yield the extraordinary if only I looked hard enough, if only I kept at it and did not give up. As best I can say it, that is the same impulse that fires my faith in God even now. Day after day I look at my life, the lives of my neighbors, the world in which we all live, and I hunt the hidden figure, the presence that still moves just beneath the surface of every created thing. Sometimes I can only make out a hand, or a foot, or an all-seeing eye, but I know it is there, even when I am not able to see it whole.

It is an imaginative enterprise, in which I must first of all give up the notion that I know what I am looking at when I look at the world. I do not know. All I know is that there is always more than meets the eye and that if I want to see truly I must be willing to look beyond the appearance of things into the depth of things, into the layers of meaning with which the least blade of grass is endowed. I must also be willing to look between things and not always at them, since a direct gaze often misses what may be glimpsed at the corner of the eye. The space between two branches may become more promising than the branches themselves; the shadows cast by a tree on the ground may hold more possibilities than the tree itself.

In order to discern the hidden figure, it is often necessary to cross your eyes or stand on your head so that all known relationships are called into question and new ones may be imagined. When earth and sky are reversed and it seems entirely plausible that lawns may grow down instead of up, then you are in a good position to glimpse the hidden figure, because you are ready to approach it on its own terms instead of your own. It is a way of seeing—a way of living—that requires a certain loosening of the grip, a willingness to be surprised, confused, amazed by the undreamt-of ways that God chooses to be revealed to us. To find the extraordinary hidden in the ordinary, we are called to participate in God's own imagination—to see ourselves, our neighbors, and our world through God's eyes, full of possibility, full of promise, ready to be transformed.

Because God is not through with us yet. At our worst moments, both individually and corporately, we act as if that were so. We act as if creation had all been finished a long, long time ago and encased in glass, where we may look at it through the grime of centuries but may not touch. Nothing could be further from the truth. The Holy Spirit still moves over the face of the waters, God still breathes life into piles of dust, Jesus still shouts us from our tombs. The deep river of revelation still runs strong from the fresh headwaters of its source to its jewel-encrusted banks in the heavenly city, with power to drench our dry days along the way.

To believe that is an act of faith, which is an imaginative act. In faith, we imagine ourselves whole, imagine ourselves in love with our neighbors, imagine ourselves bathed and fed by God, imagine the creation at peace, imagine the breath of God coinciding with our own, imagine the heart of God beating at the heart of the world. It is a vision of the kingdom, but is it true or false, fact or fiction? That is the question God continues to ask us: What *is* real to us, what is *true*, and what do we intend to do about it?

NOTES

1. James D. Whitehead, "The Religious Imagination," *Liturgy* 5 (1985), 54-59.
2. Jamake Hightower, *The Primal Mind: Vision & Reality in Indian America* (New York: Harper & Row, 1981), 75.

CHAPTER FIVE

Bible

Several years ago, a young friend of mine packed her bags and went away to college, where she intended to become a religion major. She had gotten deeply involved in the youth group at her church and was entertaining the idea of becoming an ordained minister herself, so she wasted no time enrolling in Religion 101. During the first week of classes, her mother told me, her professor introduced her to the J, E, P, and D writers of Genesis and pointed out the discrepancies between the two different creation stories in chapters one and two. Hearing all of this for the first time, my young friend put her head down on her desk and sobbed out loud.

Everyone who decides to study the Bible runs the same risk. While it is certainly possible to love Holy Scripture and even to live by it without the faintest knowledge of biblical criticism, those who decide to probe its mysteries will soon find human fingerprints all over the place. There are historical inaccuracies and outright contradictions, clumsy repetitions and obvious collations. Relics of other religious traditions lie buried in the text—like the *nephilim* of Genesis 6:4 or the council of the gods in Psalm 82:1—and such discoveries may dishearten those who encounter them for the first time. Like Dorothy in *The Wizard of Oz*, they may watch in horror as Toto grips the heavy velvet curtain in his teeth and exposes the balding old man behind the wizard's awesome facade, but those who survive the shock may press on to find that no wizard does not mean no God.

For all the human handiwork it displays, the Bible remains a peculiarly holy book. I cannot think of any other text that has such authority over me, interpreting me faster than I can interpret it. It speaks to me not with the stuffy voice of some mummified sage but with the fresh, lively tones of someone who knows what happened to me an hour ago. Familiar passages accumulate meaning as I return to them again and again. They seem to grow during my absences from them; I am always finding something new in them I never found before, something designed to meet me where I am at this particular moment in time.

This is, I believe, why we call the Bible God's "living" word. When I think about consulting a medical book thousands of years old for some insight into my health, or an equally ancient physics book for some help with my cosmology, I understand what a strange and unparalleled claim the Bible has on me. Age does not diminish its power but increases it. When I recognize my life in its pages—when I am convinced that this story is *my* story—then I am lifted out of my own time and space and set free, liberated by the knowledge that my oddly shaped piece of life is not a fluke but fits into a much larger and more reliable puzzle. In other words, I am not an orphan. I have a community, a history, a future, a God. The Bible is my birth certificate and my family tree, but it is more: it is the living vein that connects me to my maker, pumping me the stories I need to know about who we have been to one another from the beginning of time, and who we are now, and who we shall be when time is no more.

What the Bible *isn't* is a collection of stories about admirable men and women who loved and served their Lord. It is instead an encyclopedia of human life on earth, with a few saints but far more scoundrels who lied and cheated their ways into the annals of sacred history. Hearing their stories, I listen for family resemblances. Am I as trusting as Abraham, as brave as Ruth, as persistent as Paul? I flinch at family flaws. Am I as devious as Rebecca, as petulant as Jonah, as treacherous as Judas? But throughout all their stories, which are also my stories, I hear God's story, and that is something else altogether.

God's story has its own twists and turns, its own chapters of rage and repentance along with some magnificent cruelties, but it is above all the story of a God who does not break promises, a God who entered into covenant with humankind and who remains loyal to that bond, no matter what we may think of its terms and no matter how we may connive to test them. That is the God who walks toward me in the Bible—not only the God of the past but also the God of the present and the future, whose promise of relationship has no expiration date. The Bible is the book in which the terms of that relationship are explored.

It is an historic relationship. It has a particular shape and flavor to it; certain themes recur and build in a familiar way. God creates life out of darkness and chaos. We want more. God sets limits. We challenge them. God is God. We try to be God too. God judges. We get the message. God forgives. We forget the message. God keeps choosing us; we keep choosing death. God creates life out of darkness and chaos. We rejoice: "Thanks be to God!"

Ours is an historic faith. We believe in a God who acts in time, who began acting long before we came upon the scene and who will continue acting long after we are gone from it, which means that our present trust is sustained by memory on the one hand and hope on the other. Both are common property; neither is our personal possession. Faith may be an imaginative act, as I have suggested, but the Bible reminds us that we are not free to imagine anything we like. We may not imagine that God speaks only through cats, for instance, or that turning three circles before walking out the front door will protect us from harm each day. By keeping us rooted in our historical tradition, the Bible helps us to know the difference between imagination and delusion; by tethering our own imaginations to that of the whole people of God, the Bible teaches us to imagine the God who was and is and who shall be.

The Bible also teaches us how to imagine ourselves. In a world where we are offered so many unsolicited definitions of ourselves, it is easy to forget who we are. First there are all the voices that come to us from outside ourselves, describing us as successes or failures based on our looks, our performances, our incomes. According to a copy of *Vanity Fair* magazine I read recently, the ideal human being is rich, thin, powerful, and smart. If the women are not beautiful, at least they dress well, while the men tend toward a look of dishevelled aristocracy. Children, oddly enough, are nowhere to be seen.

Then there are the voices that come to us from inside ourselves, reminding us what we will never be, never do, never have. No one has ever explained to my satisfaction where this relentlessly critical chorus comes from, but it never seems to tire of telling me how clumsy, lazy, weak, spoiled, thick-headed, ridiculous, and doomed to failure I am. There are some days when it all sounds true, but there are others when I recognize the voice of the Tempter and am able to fight back. You have overstated your case, I am able to say; you have gone too far. While there is a splinter of truth in all your accusations, you have missed the central truth: God made me, and God does not make trash.

How do I know that? Because the Bible tells me so. The Bible tells me that God can make a human being out of a pile of dirt, that God can make a barren old couple the proud parents of a chosen people, that God can heal the sick and feed the hungry and raise the dead. If I believe that, then I cannot also believe myself or anyone else to be a lost cause. Nor can I believe only what my culture tells me about myself. The Bible gives me another authority to consult. When the culture treats me as if all I am good for is to produce or to consume, the Bible invites me to love. When the culture encourages me to think of myself as a rugged individualist, the Bible calls me to be a neighbor. When the culture conditions me to become a spectator on life, the Bible bids me to do justice, and love mercy, and walk humbly with my God. Over and over, the Bible offers me an alternative vision, not only of myself but also of other people and ultimately of the whole world. Sometimes it seems farfetched, but other times it seems truer than what is supposed to be true.

A few years ago I spent a month in Israel, arriving in Tel Aviv one day after Saddam Hussein invaded Kuwait. Tension between Palestinians and Israelis was running high; their mutual fear and hatred hung over the streets of Jerusalem like toxic smog. I saw Palestinian boys throw stones at Jewish tourists and Israeli soldiers smash bottles all through the Muslim quarter of the Old City. The Arabs went on strike every afternoon, closing their shops and withdrawing behind shut doors. City authorities retaliated by withholding municipal services, so that many Palestinian neighborhoods were covered with uncollected garbage.

During my last week in Jerusalem, I walked through one such neighborhood with a small group of Christians. We were on the traditional pilgrims' route that leads from Bethany down the Mount of Olives to the ancient garden of Gethsemane. We were imagining Jesus ahead of us, balanced on the back of a small donkey, entering the last week of his life along a road strewn with palms. Arab children joined us as we went, while their mothers watched us from darkened doorways and windows. Just before descending to Gethsemane we paused at a rise in the road to look across the Kidron Valley at Jerusalem. We looked at it with some of the heartache Jesus must have felt, caught between its beauty and its violence. On our side of the valley, the barren hillside was covered with trash. Skinny dogs sniffed empty tin cans while the August wind caught stray wrappers and sent them crackling out of sight. On the other side of the valley all we could see were graves. The western slope of the Mount of Olives is covered with graves, because everyone wants to be there to meet the Messiah when he comes.

Silenced by the scenery, we hardly noticed the sheets our leader put into our hands, inviting us to read Isaiah 60.1-5 together. "Arise, shine; for your light has come," we read in unison, "and the glory of the Lord has risen upon you." It was preposterous. There was no correspondence between what we were seeing and what we were saying. "For darkness shall cover the earth, and thick darkness the peoples; but the Lord will arise upon you, and his glory will appear over you. Nations shall come to your light, and kings to the brightness of your dawn." The disparity between the vision and the reality was wrenching, like looking at a wasteland through a window painted with flowers. As we continued to read, however, my eyes began to play tricks on me. "Lift up your eyes and look around," Isaiah dared me, and the land before me became transparent. Instead of a garbage dump, I saw a holy city, with pilgrims streaming to it from the four corners of the earth. "They all gather together, they come to you; your sons shall come from far away, and your daughters shall be carried on their nurses' arms." It was not a lie; the reality had not yet caught up with God's vision, but it would. The Bible told me so.

While it is certainly possible to experience this kind of revelation simply by opening the Bible and reading what you find there, my own experience has taught me the value of regular and intentional study. My relationship with the Bible is not a romance but a marriage, and one I am willing to work on in all the usual ways: by living with the text day in and day out, by listening to it and talking back to it, by making sure I know what is behind the words it speaks to me and being certain I have heard it properly, by refusing to distance myself from the parts of it I do not like or understand, by letting my love for it show up in the everyday acts of my life. The Bible is not an object for me; it is a partner, whose presence blesses me, challenges me, and affects everything I do.

My first serious study of the Bible began in seminary, where I read Genesis in Hebrew and discovered a whole new world. Each day's vocabulary list opened new windows. Adam got his name from *adamah*, the dust of the earth. At least one of the words for God, *elohim*, was plural.

The word for "eye" also meant "fountain of water," and the word for "rib" could also be interpreted "side room," which told me that Eve was created from one whole side of Adam's nature. I thought I was the first person in the world to discern that Isaac's name came from the root word for laughter, his mother Sarah's snort of incredulity and joy when the angels predicted his birth.

After that, I was hooked. I could not read the simplest passage in the Old or New Testaments without wondering what the words really meant. I found acrostic psalms that read like crossword puzzles in Hebrew and puns that were audible only in Greek. My whole understanding of Jesus' humanity changed when I learned that his having "compassion" for the crowds who were like sheep without a shepherd meant that his very bowels turned over inside of him. For the first time I began to pay attention to the dissimilarities between the four gospels, wondering why each of them told Jesus' story in a different way. Why did Mark and John skip the birth stories? Why did Matthew leave out the shepherds, and why did Luke leave out the wise men from the East? Why were the last words John and Luke put on Jesus' lips different from Matthew's and Mark's?

The more I discovered what was there, the more I discovered what was not. Adam and Eve ate "forbidden fruit" in Eden, but nowhere in the Bible is an apple mentioned. Jacob made a long-sleeved robe for his favorite son Joseph, not a coat of many colors. Matthew describes travelers from the East who bore gifts to Bethlehem, but "We Three Kings" is pure invention. All of this excited me, because there was clearly much more to the Bible than I had ever expected, and exploring it demanded more of me as well. I did not have to settle for memorizing the books of the Old Testament in order or reciting key passages from John. I could take the text apart and put it back together again without harming it, ask questions and challenge the answers without being struck by lightning. The word of God turned out to be plenty strong enough to withstand my curiosity. Every time I poked it, it poked me back. Every time I wrenched it around so I could see inside, it sprang back into shape the moment I was through. In short, the Bible turned out not to be a fossil under glass but a thousand different things—a mirror, a scythe, a hammock, a lantern, a pair of binoculars, a high diving board, a bridge, a goad—all of them offering themselves to me to be touched and handled and used.

The fine southern novelist Reynolds Price did his own translation of the four gospels a few years back and called the book *A Palpable God.* I shelve my copy next to my Bibles, to remind me how lucky I am. Our God could be an ethereal God, after all, a disembodied deity whose holy word was a collection of abstract philosophical premises. Instead, we have a God who is pleased to dwell among us, setting the holy story within the human story so that none of us has to leave flesh and blood behind to hear it. We do not have to park our bodies outside before entering God's presence. God is willing to meet us where we are, coming among us as a burning bush, a mighty wind, a pillar of cloud, a still small voice, a descending dove, a newborn babe.

The Bible's great good news is that God is a palpable God, whose presence can be sniffed and glimpsed in every corner of creation. There are no yellow and black striped lines in the Bible separating sacred territory from secular. "Remove the sandals from your feet," God tells Moses in the middle of nowhere, "for the place on which you are standing is holy ground" (Exod. 3:5). God's presence is all that is required to turn ordinary desert sand into the Holy of Holies, or a straw-stuffed manger into the birthplace of the Lord. As Jacob learned on the road to Haran, there is a well-traveled ladder between heaven and earth that has a way of touching down wherever we happen to be. "Surely the Lord is in this place—and I did not know it!" he exclaimed, rising from his stone pillow to wipe the sleep from his eyes. "How awesome is this place! This is none other than the house of God, and this is the gate of heaven" (Gen. 28:16-17).

Jacob set up a pillar before he left and gave his awesome place a name—Bethel, "house of God"—but in doing so he may have missed the point, because God does not stay put.

Bethel is everywhere; the gate of heaven is always right in front of us. If pillars marked all the places in the world where God has come among us, we could not move without cracking our shins.

This is good news, although some of God's epiphanies are more welcome than others. The God who created heaven and earth is also the God who sent the flood, and the God who parted the Red Sea is the same one who ordered Abraham to slit Isaac's throat. If the Bible is not a book about admirable men and women, neither is it a book about a conventionally admirable God. It is a book in which wonderful and terrible things happen by the power of an *almighty* God, whose steadfast love for us does not seem to preclude scaring the living daylights out of us from time to time.

People who claim to have no fear of the Lord have clearly not read the Bible. Someone needs to sit them down with a selected reading list that includes the ten plagues sent upon Egypt, the murder of Sisera, the slaughter of the Amalekites and the prophets of Baal, and perhaps the mauling of forty-two boys by two she-bears in the name of the Lord. If they protest that these are stories about what God does to *bad* people, then they should read the book of Job straight through, and if they insist that their God is the God of the New Testament, then they should study the passion narratives in each of the four gospels and see what happens to those who obey the will of God. We can run but we can't hide: if early death on a cross is how God rewards a well-beloved son who knows no sin, then what hope is there for the rest of us?

In C. S. Lewis' classic children's book, *The Lion, the Witch and the Wardrobe,* a large lion named Aslan pads around the edges of the story, appearing at strategic moments to save four lost children from danger and guide them home. Hearing about him for the first time from a couple of friendly beavers, the children have doubts about whether they are looking forward to meeting him.

"Is he—quite safe?" asks one of the girls. "I shall feel rather nervous about meeting a lion."

> "That you will, dearie, and no mistake," said Mrs. Beaver, "if there's anyone who can appear before Aslan without their knees knocking, they're either braver than most or else just silly."
> "Then he isn't safe?" said Lucy.
> "Safe?" said Mr. Beaver. "Don't you hear what Mrs. Beaver tells you? Who said anything about safe? 'Course he isn't safe. But he's good. He's the King, I tell you."[1]

It is a statement of faith, based on experience. The King is not safe. The King is sovereign, which means that he is frightening, because his subjects have no control over him. He does not ask their advice before he acts. He is no one's pet. His rescue of them may be as hair-raising as what he is rescuing them from, but he is good, which means that he can be trusted. If they will just press through their fear of him, he will save them. If they will just climb on his back as he tells them to and hang on for dear life, he will carry them home.

Believing in the God of the Bible calls for the same kind of faith. While there is plenty for us to fear, there is also plenty for us to hope. The God who does not break promises can be trusted to go on creating the world out of darkness and chaos, putting breath into our dust and dry bones, turning our lives and deaths inside out in order to set us free. We may not always approve of God's methods, but fortunately our approval is not required. God will save us anyhow, if we will just stay out of the way.

Biblical faith gives believers a particular pattern by which to judge the truth of their own experience. We see that service may be the way to greatness, poverty may be the key to freedom, weakness may be the path to strength, death may be the gate to life. The Bible confirms all these suspicions, and while it may not make them any easier for us to act upon, at least it gives us courage to go on when everything seems stacked against us. For those rooted in Christian memory and fed by Christian hope, nothing in life is simply what it seems. Equipped with the paradoxical images and stories of our historic faith, we see things differently than we would without them.

One of the hardest things I do is to celebrate communion at a local nursing home on the poor side of town, where most residents spend their days strapped in wheelchairs against the walls of the television room. Once a month, nurses roll ten or fifteen of them into the sun room and park them in a semicircle around a small table. Some of them complain as I prepare the elements—"Get me out of here! Take me back to my room right now!"—while others doze or stare or drool. Few stay awake through the whole twenty-minute service. When it is time for them to take communion I go from chair to chair, patting them awake and asking them if they want the bread and wine. About half let me press the elements to their lips; the rest refuse to be roused or else they look at me as if I am a burglar. It is one of the hardest things I do because I sometimes doubt the power of the sacrament to break through their fog. I say all the comfortable words and wonder if anyone hears them. I stand there with my arms raised over the bread and wine and suspect that I might as well be flying a kite.

The last time I went was late on a Monday afternoon. One of the volunteers warned me that everyone's medication was wearing off, which was a mixed blessing. My congregation were more awake than usual, but they were also more vocal. I could hardly make myself heard over the din in the room. One woman sang, "Row, row, row your boat" throughout the beginning of the service, bouncing so hard against her restraints that her chair lurched toward me as I read the opening prayers. In a bid for attention, I clapped my hands and asked them to choose the gospel lesson for the day.

"What shall I read from the Bible this afternoon?" I asked them. "What part would you like to hear?" The commotion lessened long enough for one old woman's broken voice to be heard above it.

"Tell us a resurrection story," she said. I never saw who it was, but as her words settled down over the room the movers and shakers held still for a moment and the sleepers opened their eyes.

"Yes," someone else said, and then someone else. "Yes. Tell us a resurrection story."

The Bible tells us the stories we need and want to hear— stories to help us live, stories to help us die, and stories to help us believe we shall live again. Listening to them, we are called into relationship with the One who tells them to us. Believing them, we are changed. The living words of God heal our hurts and soften our hearts; they clear our vision and guide our feet. Like a lifeline strung from the beginning of time to the end, they show us a way through all the storms of culture, nature, and history. They show us the way to the Word beyond all our words, in whose presence we shall be made eloquent at last.

NOTES
1. C.S. Lewis, *The Lion, the Witch, and the Wardrobe* (New York: Macmillan, 1950), 75-76.

CHAPTER SIX

Worship

At the last church I served, it was traditional to stage a dramatic reading of the Palm Sunday narrative on the Sunday before Easter. The solemn occasion began with the announcement of the gospel. Then the lights went down and even the children in the congregation fell silent as the red-robed participants moved into their places. The principal readers stood spotlit in the chancel, but other players were seated throughout the dark church beside unsuspecting parishioners. The only prop was a ten-foot-tall cross made of rough wood that towered at the top of the chancel steps, draped with a blood-red stole and full of splinters.

On the Sunday I am remembering, the drama had built steadily toward its dreaded conclusion. Jesus stood in front of the cross with his head bowed as Pilate addressed the crowd. "Then what should I do with Jesus who is called the Messiah?" he asked us. Players leapt to their feet in the dark pews. "Crucify him!" they shrieked, one after the other, their fury erupting like hot geysers throughout the congregation. "Let him be crucified!"

Come fully to life, the story was awful. It was always awful, but those of us who had endured it before knew that it would soon be over. Hunching our shoulders against what was to come, we were waiting for the end when a strange, new voice began to make itself heard over the din. "Oh my

Lord, no!" wailed an unrehearsed woman's voice. "Don't kill my sweet Jesus! You've got to stop! You can't kill my sweet Jesus! O Lord, make them stop!"

The ushers at the back of the church peered into the darkness, trying to find where the voice was coming from. The one nearest her finally located her and sat down beside her, as people all around her patted her and whispered to her. Accepting their offer of a cup of coffee, she let them lead her out of the church just as Jesus gave up his spirit with a heart-splitting howl.

She had wandered in off the street, as it turned out, still high from the night before, and had taken a seat without knowing what was about to occur. "I tried to tell her it wasn't real," said a teenaged girl who was sitting next to her, "but I realized that, for her, it was."

Worship is the ongoing practice of faith, and not only the practice but the actual experience of it. Whether it takes place around a kitchen table or the carved marble altar of a great cathedral, worship is how the people of God practice their reliance on their Lord. Through liturgies of word and table—"liturgy" meaning "the work of the people"—we do what we were created to do. We pray, we listen to God's word, we confess, we make peace, we lift up our hearts, we hold out our hands, we are fed, we give thanks, we go forth. We practice the patterns of our life together before God, rehearsing them until they become second nature to us. In the liturgy of the word, we come to understand that the God who has been involved with us since time began is involved with us still. In the liturgy of the table, we experience the incarnate Lord who feeds and forgives and calls us to follow him into the world. Through both of these encounters we expand our images of what it means to be human and what it means to be divine, so that we are better able to live into the fullness of our heritage as sons and daughters of God.

We bring all of who we are to worship. It is a bodily experience and not one for our spirits alone. There are faces to be looked at, voices to be heard, hands to be touched, bread to be tasted, and wine to be smelled. We sing things we could just as easily say and bow when we say other things, some of us touching ourselves gently on forehead, chest, and shoulders as if we were tracing a cross. Sometimes we kneel, assuming a posture that is all but gone from our world—like troubadours, like lovers, like servants, we kneel before the Lord our maker and our hearts follow suit. Then we stand to sing and sit to listen, dancing the peculiar ballet of the people of God.

Our worship is the medium of our identity over time. Like a family album, our liturgy bears the marks of those who have gone before us—portraits of those we have never met, inscriptions written in many different hands, bits and pieces of treasured correspondence, favorite recipes, prayers, and remedies—all of them left for us by our ancestors in the faith, who have bequeathed us their manual for approaching God.

In my case, that manual is the Book of Common Prayer. In it, I can find prayers for every occasion along with personal and corporate patterns of worship for morning, noon, and night. Holding it in my hands and praying from it, I take my place in the long line of those who have done so before me. I hear them praying the same or similar words with me, with historical accents that reach all the way back to first-century Palestine. "Lift up your hearts," the celebrant says, and we all toss our hearts in the air, ignorant of the centuries that separate us.

A couple of summers ago I found myself in a small, tin-roofed church in western Kenya, just a few miles away from the Ugandan border. There was no glass in the cinderblock windows. Carpenter bees flew in and out with their loud engines while chickens clucked and pecked for seeds outside. The congregation sat cross-legged on the swept dirt floor, nursing children and swatting flies. In front of them stood the altar, a battered kitchen table adorned with wild flowers in old shortening cans and two precious beeswax candles. A marmalade cat slept underneath, oblivious to the crowd.

The occasion was baptism, and while everything was strange to me it was also familiar, because I knew the pattern. First the vicar led the congregation in songs and prayers. Then he invited the mothers to bring their children forward. One by one they knelt in front of him as he took a baby in his arms, named the child, and dipped his hand into the large enamel soup pot that was the baptismal font. Then he doused the child three times, making the sign of the cross on its forehead as the waters of baptism soaked into the brown dirt below. I did not understand a word of the service, but I understood perfectly what we were doing that morning. I had learned it halfway around the world in another language, including the part that begins, "We believe in one God...."

Essentially mysterious but entirely accessible, the sacraments are pure genius for teaching us what we need to know and, paradoxically, what we can never know about our relationship with God. By giving us seven formal sacraments, the church gives us seven patterns for approaching that relationship. While baptism and eucharist remain the primary patterns for the Christian life—the two great celebrations of acceptance and belonging—still the sacraments of confirmation, ordination, marriage, penance, and healing also have things to teach us whether we participate in them directly or not. In every case, the first thing they teach us is that we do not worship God alone. We need other people in our lives to feed us and forgive us, to touch us and bless us and strengthen our resolve. There are no solo sacraments. We need one another.

The second thing sacraments teach us is that God uses material things to reach out to us. Sacramental worship is nothing less than worship of the God who is in our midst, present to us in bread and wine, water and oil, in hands and feet and kisses of peace. If, in touching or being touched by these ordinary things, we believe that we are being touched by God, then we can no longer draw a clear line between the secular and the sacred in our lives. Every created thing is a potential messenger, sent to teach us more about our relationship with God.

The third thing sacraments teach us is that God is not delicate. The sacraments of the church are not weekend performances in sacred settings; they are portable. The sacraments of the church may take place in prison cells, intensive care units, nursing homes, halfway houses, night shelters, AIDS clinics, and anywhere else the people of God decide to carry them, including corporate headquarters and the steps of city hall. No place that is human is too messy for God. The sacraments teach us to seek God's presence at all times and in all places. They belong to the world, and not only to the church.

Those of us who learn them in church learn things we carry out into the world with us when we go, things that affect the way we live the rest of our lives. Whether we are witnesses or participants, the sacraments reveal the deep patterns of God's relationship with us, showing us the ways in which God is willing to cleanse, strengthen, inspire, empower, bless, forgive, feed, and heal those who come to God in faith. Sometimes there are requirements. The sacraments of baptism and ordination include lengthy examinations; the sacrament of marriage involves solemn vows. The sacrament of penance obliges penitents to confess their sins and amend their lives.

The sacrament of ministration to the sick, on the other hand, is pure grace. To receive God's unction all you have to do is lie there, which is a sacramental way of reminding us that God's healing presence is God's free gift to us and nothing we can earn. This is true, in fact, of all the sacraments, whether or not they require things of us. In them, we may prepare our hearts and learn our parts in order to enter the presence of the Lord, but in the end our best efforts are beside the point. Like the prodigal son's loving father, God is out the door to greet us before we can get our strangled speeches out of our mouths, bestowing on us the very relationship for which we were ready to beg. This does not render sacraments unnecessary, however; the prodigal had to find his way home. In order to reclaim his father's love he had to leave the far country of his self-banishment and remember where he came from. He had to show up to receive the gift.

Sacraments are our road maps home. God may not need them, but we do, and while they cannot make something happen, at least they make sure that we are in the right place if it should. Sacraments work, but it is hard to say how. They change lives, but it is hard to say why. The difficulty may lie in their proximity to the holy. Sacraments lead us directly into the precincts of heaven, which the language of earth has always found tricky to describe. "Oh," may be the best we can do, or "yes," or "thank you," or "amen."

The great coming-home sacrament of all time is the eucharist, the only one of the seven given to us directly by our Lord. In it, all the other sacraments are represented: we are forgiven, strengthened, healed, blessed, fed, and sent forth in a rite that sets us apart as God's people in the world. Whether we take part in a quiet thirty-minute service with seven other people or a full festal celebration in a packed church, the eucharistic map remains the same. Step by step, it leads us into the presence and very being of God, where holy flesh and blood become our own.

At every step, we practice some discipline of the church. From the opening acclamation to the dismissal, every element of the service has something to teach us about our life with God and one another. Practicing them over and over again, we build up the muscles of our hearts, souls, and minds, exercising our ability to respond to the presence of the holy in our midst.

The service opens with the declaration of a truth about God. Depending on the season of the church year, it is about the blessedness of God, or the risenness of Christ, or the enduring mercy of the Lord. By starting in this way, we state clearly whom we worship and why. We name the end of our journey as we begin and carry it with us, a banner curling above our heads as we go. Then we pray the collect for purity, announcing our willingness to be known by the God from whom no secrets are hid. It is an intentional surrender on our parts, a dropping of defenses that says we would not hide if we could. It also reminds us that we may not seek the revelation of God without being revealed ourselves. Praying the collect for purity, we stand stripped before God, naked and ready to be cleansed.

The gloria, the kyrie eleison, or the trisagion follow, further defining our relationship to the one we worship, and then we hear the collect of the day. While the prayer book contains hundreds of collects, as various as the occasions upon which they are prayed, each ends in the same way, by acclaiming our Lord Jesus Christ, "who lives and reigns with you and the Holy Spirit, one God, now and forever, Amen." Like small magnets that align our sensibilities, the collects point us in the right direction and put our hands in the hand of the only one who can show us the way.

Then we come to the lessons appointed for the day—one, two, or three of them—along with a psalm. By following the lectionary, we submit ourselves to one of the most ancient disciplines of the church. Instead of picking and choosing our own ways through the Bible, we consent to take a guided walk. With regular stops in the Old and New Testaments, it is a path that expands our horizons. Frequently it leads us into territory we would never thought to have entered or would have preferred to avoid, but that is the beauty of the walk. We do not select the parts of Scripture we hear any more than we select the daily events of our lives. Both are given, and by accepting both we learn to look for God in everything that comes our way and not only in the things we like. "Thanks be to God." That is how we are asked to respond to the reading of Scripture, whether it brings welcome news or gruesome. We do not say it because we approve of what we have heard or even because we agree with it. We say it because we believe that God is in it somehow and that God is for us.

After the lessons comes the sermon. While celebrants have been known to omit it from time to time and their congregations have been known to appreciate the gesture, the prayer book gives no indication that the sermon is optional. The reason for that, I think, is that the word of God calls for a response with some human daring in it. Certainly there are ways in which the rest of the service constitutes our response to the gospel, but the words of the liturgy are theologically correct words that stay the same from week to week. A sermon, on the other hand, is an act of creation with real risk in it, as one foolhardy human being presumes to address both God and humankind, speaking to each on the other's behalf and praying to get out of the pulpit alive.

For the preacher, the discipline of the sermon is to respond to the word of God as one who represents both God and the people of God. For the congregation, the discipline of the sermon is to listen to one person's interpretation of the word in order to learn how it is done, because a good sermon does not stop when the preacher sits down, but goes on posing questions and evoking responses long after it is over. The congregation's job is not simply to accept—or ignore—what a sermon says, but to wrestle with the same passages of Scripture the preacher is wrestling with until God's word yields its particular blessing for each one of them. Nor is it the preacher's job to send people home with good advice ringing in their ears, but with the tools they need to discern God's voice speaking to them in the particular circumstances of their own lives.

Sermons are like any other human inventions: sometimes they work and sometimes they don't, which is why it is a wise move to go from the sermon directly to the creed. There, in story form, we recite the summary of our faith in words the church has used for hundreds and hundreds of years. They are so familiar to our ears that most of us say them in our sleep, forgetting the bloody battles waged over each of them, the lives lost as heresy after heresy was hammered out of the creed.

All the hard mysteries of the faith are embedded there: the triune God, the virgin birth, the last judgment, the resurrection of the dead. A friend of mine, a professional singer who performs sacred works all over the world, recently asked for my help. She has sung masses by all the great composers. She knows the liturgy of the church by heart and suffers most of its mysteries gladly, but the credo still sticks in her mind like a splinter. "Do you have anything you can give me," she asked, "that explains the middle section of the creed?"

All I could give her was what I give myself—the reassurance that the creed is said in the plural, not the singular. When I say, "We believe..." I count on that to cover what I cannot believe on my own right now. When my faith limps, I lean on the faith of the church, letting "our" faith suffice until "mine" returns. Later, when I am able to say, "We believe..." with renewed confidence, I know that I am filling in for others who are indisposed for the time being, as they filled in for me. My decision to say the creed at all is a decision to trust those who have gone before me, embracing the faith they have commended to me.

The prayers of the people expand that "we" even more. By praying not only for the universal church but also for the welfare of the whole world, the people of God discover that "us" includes every created thing. We pray for those we have never met along with those we love. We pray for those who will not or cannot pray for themselves. We pray for the earth and its creatures; we pray for our enemies; we pray for the living and the dead. We become intercessors for the entire web of being to which we belong and in doing so we act like the priests we are, offering the whole world back to God in prayer.

We confess our sins in the same way. We do not kneel as individuals, turning a private laundry list of sins over to God, but as the body of Christ, to confess the ways in which all humanity has missed the mark set for us, failing to love God with our whole hearts, failing to love our neighbors as ourselves. A remnant of the whole cloth, we confess on behalf of all those who are created in God's image, ourselves included, and we ask for God's mercy and forgiveness upon us all. We are absolved not once in our lives, nor twice, but regularly. We need the renewing power of God's forgiveness as much as we need food or water or air. If there is shame in this, it is redeeming shame, because it reminds us who we

are meant to be and who, by the grace of God, we are becoming.

The exchange of the peace, during which we greet one
another in the name of the Lord, signifies to us the communal nature of our worship. For some people it is a horrible
moment in which the slow beauty of the service is interrupted for a square dance. I will never forget one venerable
old gentleman I used to sit behind who dropped to his knees
the moment the peace was announced and stayed there, his
gnarled hands clasped high above his head, until the storm
had passed. He had a point. The peace can be a noisy, awkward, unruly moment, but that is how people are when the
Holy Spirit blows through our midst. Whether or not we
sprout flames above our heads, we can set up quite a racket.

The peace also signals the shift as we move from the liturgy of the word to the liturgy of the table. The logical left
brain is just about through with its work; it is the right
brain's turn to train its powers of imagination and intuition
on what cannot be grasped in any other way. The action
moves past the pulpit to the altar. Bread and wine are pre-
sented. Candles are lit. The hands of the celebrant become
hovering birds, spreading their wings over the gleam of polished silver and white linen. Time is measured by what they
do: now it is time to touch the elements; now it is time to
sign them with the cross; now it is time to break the bread;
now it is time to lift the cup. A deep silence settles down.
Even the words that are spoken have silence in them, as the
celebrant takes, blesses, breaks, and gives us the food that
sustains our lives.

It is a pattern we learned first on a hillside in Galilee, at a
holy picnic where the first eucharist took place. Faced with
the hunger of five thousand people, Jesus took five loaves
and two fish, blessed them, broke them, and gave them
away, initiating a fourfold pattern he would repeat at least
twice more in his life—once around a supper table and once
on a cross, where he took, blessed, broke, and gave the saving bread of his own body and the dark burgundy of his
blood.

This is the meal we reach out for at the communion rail, caught between our desire to be fed and our certain knowledge that we too are being called to take, bless, break, and give the stuff of our own lives. Children tend to understand the paradox better than their parents. One small girl I know reached out for the cup of her first communion, eager to taste what was inside. Her chubby fingers circled the chalice as she peered into her reflection.

"The blood of Christ," I said, guiding it to her lips, "the cup of salvation."

"Yuck!" she said, pushing the cup back at me. "You keep it. I don't want any."

Her reaction made perfect sense. Who willingly drinks human blood or eats human flesh? The taboo against dining on members of our own species is strong and old. In biblical times, consuming body and blood was something reserved for one's worst enemies, as when the psalmist writes, "When evildoers assail me to devour my flesh—my adversaries and foes—they shall stumble and fall" (Ps. 27:2). Christ's instructions to his disciples to do just that have left Christians vulnerable to ridicule by those outside the faith and to doubt by those inside. What can it mean, to call bread flesh and wine blood? More urgently, what can it mean to swallow them as a way of communing with our Lord?

Late last summer the lectionary stalled for a long time in the sixth chapter of John, where Jesus baffles the multitudes by feeding them on five barley loaves and two dried fish, and then by speaking of himself as the bread from heaven. For three whole weeks he kept after us: "I am the bread of life; he who comes to me shall not hunger, and he who believes in me shall never thirst" (6:35). "I am the living bread which came down from heaven; if anyone eats of this bread, he will live forever; and the bread which I shall give for the life of the world is my flesh" (6:51). "Do you take offence at this?" (6:61).

While I was mulling it all over, I spent some time with my new goddaughter Madeline. Just three months old, she lived her life in her mother's arms, comforted by the familiar sounds and smells of the one-person universe into which she had been born. She slept, she woke, she fed at her mother's breast, finding everything she needed in that one nourishing embrace. Watching her nurse one day, I saw that her mother was truly her food, the body and blood from which her own flesh had been made and from which she daily accepted her life as a matter of course. "He who eats my flesh and drinks my blood abides in me, and I in him" (John 6:56).

What are we to believe? When Jesus invites us to his meal, is it an invitation to a picnic, a blood sacrifice, a last supper, a turn at God's breast? We are not invited to understand; we are simply invited to be fed, holding out our hands to receive what it has pleased God to put into them. Like holy manna, it is not the meal we had planned nor even the meal we would have thought to want, but it is the meal God has given us, the very bread of heaven.

The prayer after communion is our thank-you note. In it, we praise God for showing us such gracious hospitality, but we also recognize that we have been fed for a reason. "Send us now into the world in peace," we pray. "Send us out to do the work you have given us to do." This holy meal is not Eggs Benedict and champagne cocktails for heaven's executives; it is a stack of buckwheat hotcakes and a beaker of cold milk for her day laborers, giving us the calories we need to do the work God has given us to do.

"Go in peace to love and serve the Lord." That is the job description. Having practiced our priesthood in worship, we go forth to exercise it in our lives, loving and serving the Lord who plays hide-and-seek with us in every face we meet. "Let us go forth into the world, rejoicing in the power of the Spirit." The dismissal sentence changes our direction. It grabs us by the shoulders and turns us around, tugging us away from the lovely altar and pointing us toward an open door. At first it looks like the door out of the church, but as we walk through it we discover that it is the door into the world, where Christ may yet be found and followed. The last thing we say sums up our response to such good news: "Thanks be to God."

When I was a little girl, like many little girls I took ballet lessons. The paraphernalia was fascinating to me: the satin slippers, the stiff net tutu, the pink tights. It would have suited me to spend the whole hour admiring myself in front of the mirror, but my teacher kept insisting that I come away from there to learn the basic positions essential to ballet. Under her tutelage, I learned to bend my feet this way and that, sometimes straining so hard I feared my knees would pop from their sockets. I arched my back, I held my head up, I made perfect O's with my arms. I stretched and sweated over the positions until my bones ached and my muscles yelled out loud. Then one day I got to put them all together, bending and rising and sweeping the air like someone to whom gravity no longer applied. I got to dance.

That memory sustains me in worship, where I practice the basic positions of faith. They are named gloria, kyrie, credo, sanctus. They are named the prayers of the people, the peace, the breaking of the bread. Each one requires my full attention and best efforts; each one teaches me a particular way to move, so that when God invites me to put them all together, I may jump with joy to join the dance.

CHAPTER SEVEN

Preaching

W atching a preacher climb into the pulpit is a lot like watching a tightrope walker climb onto the platform as the drum roll begins. The first clears her throat and spreads out her notes; the second loosens his shoulders and stretches out one rosin-soled foot to test the taut rope. Then both step out into the air, trusting everything they have done to prepare for this moment as they surrender themselves to it, counting now on something beyond themselves to help them do what they love and fear and most want to do. If they reach the other side without falling, it is skill but it is also grace—a benevolent God's decision to let these daredevils tread the high places where ordinary mortals have the good sense not to go.

No other modern public speaker does what the preacher tries to do. The trial attorney has glossy photographs and bagged evidence to hand around; the teacher has blackboards and overhead projectors; the politician has brass bands and media consultants. All the preacher has is words. Climbing into the pulpit without props or sound effects, the preacher speaks—for ten or twenty or thirty minutes—to people who are used to being communicated with in very different ways. Most of the messages in our culture are sent and received in thirty seconds or less and no image on a television screen lasts more than twenty, yet a sermon requires sustained and focused attention. If the topic is not appealing, there are no other channels to be tried. If a phrase is missed, there is no replay button to be pressed. The sermon counts on listeners who will stay tuned to a message that takes time to introduce, develop, and bring to a conclusion. Listeners, for their part, count on a sermon that will not waste the time they give to it.

This is only one of many ways in which the sermon proves to be a communal act, not the creation of one person but the creation of a body of people for whom and to whom one of them speaks. A congregation can make or break a sermon by the quality of their response to it. An inspired sermon can wind up skewered somewhere near the second pew by a congregation of people who sit with their arms crossed and their eyes narrowed, coughing and scuffing their feet as the preacher struggles to be heard. Similarly, a weak sermon can grow strong in the presence of people who attend carefully to it, leaning forward in their pews and opening their faces to a preacher from whom they clearly expect to receive good news.

If the preacher is also their priest and pastor, then the sermon is theirs in another way. The quality of their life together—the memories, conversations, experiences, and hopes they share—is the fabric from which the sermon is made. The preacher is their parson, their representative person, who never gets into the pulpit without them. Whatever else the sermon is about, it is first of all about them, because they are the community in whose midst the preacher stands. In a very real way, the preacher would have no voice without them. By calling someone to preach to them and by listening to that person week after week, a congregation gives their minister both the authority to speak and a relationship from which to speak, so that every sermon begins and ends with them.

If that sounds too narrow, let me say that I also believe every sermon begins and ends with God. Because the word of God is what a preacher wrestles with in the pulpit, and because it is a living word, every sermon is God's creation as well as the creation of the preacher and the congregation.

All three participate in the making of it, with the preacher as their designated voice. It is a delicate job for the one in the pulpit, a balancing act between the text, the congregation, and the self. If the preacher leans too far one way, he will side with the text against the congregation and deliver a finger-pointing sermon from on high. If the preacher leans too far the other way, she will side with the congregation against the text and deliver a sermon that stops short of encountering God.

What is called for, instead, is a sermon that honors all of its participants, in which preachers speak in their own voices out of their own experience, addressing God on the congregation's behalf and—with great care and humility—the congregation on God's behalf. When I preach sometimes I feel like Cyrano de Bergerac in the pulpit, passing messages between two would-be lovers who want to get together but do not know how. The words are my own, but I do not speak for myself. Down in the bushes with a congregation who have elected me to speak for them, I try to put their longing into words, addressing the holy vision that appears on the moonlit balcony above our heads. Then the vision replies, and it is my job to repeat what I have heard, bringing the message back to the bushes for a response. As a preacher I am less a principal player than a go-between, a courier who serves both partners in this ancient courtship.

But I am also in love myself, which means that I am deeply involved in the messages I bear. I do not speak for myself, but I do. I am one of the crowd down in the bushes, and the longing I put into words is my own. When the holy vision speaks, it is my own heart that is pierced. While I may struggle to make sure that my response is true to those whom I represent, I cannot stay out of it myself. Every word I choose, every image, every rise in my voice reveals my own involvement in the message. That is why I have never understood preachers who claim to "stay out of" their sermons, preaching the word of God and the word of God alone. It is not possible, but there is no reason why it should be.

By choosing Christ to flesh out the word, God made a lasting decision in favor of incarnation. Those of us who are his body in the world need not shy away from the fact that our own flesh and blood continue to be where the word of God is made known. We are living libraries of God's word. Our stories are God's stories. Sometimes they are comedies and sometimes they are tragedies; sometimes faith shines through them and other times they end in darkness, but every one of them bears witness to the truth of God's word. Preachers cannot "stay out of" their sermons any more than singers can stay out of their songs. Our words are embodied, which means we bring all that we are to their expression.

But this does not mean we are free to turn the sermon into personal show-and-tell time. Those of us who preach do so as representatives. We speak as members of a body and not for ourselves alone, which means that we may not dominate the sermon any more than we may be absent from it. When I speak out of my humanity, I want my listeners to recognize their own. When I say "I" from the pulpit, I want them to say, "Me too." The sermon is no place for a virtuoso performance; it is a place for believers to explore together their common experience before God. The stories I tell from the pulpit are not just "my" stories but "our" stories, which are God's stories too. The stool of my sermon rests evenly on those three legs. If any one of them is missing (or too long or too short), the whole thing will wobble and fall.

Preaching is, above all else, an act of faith. Every time I put a sermon together, I rehearse the reasons why and the ways in which I believe in God. Given the world we live in, the case cannot be made too often. Most of us would be hard pressed on Sunday morning to say whether we are in church because we believe or because we want to believe. Like the father of the epileptic boy in Mark's gospel, we do both: "I believe; help my unbelief!" (9:24). The preacher balances on the round top of that semicolon along with the rest of the world. I cannot preach without belief, but neither can I preach without some experience of unbelief. Both are built into the human experience of the divine, and each tests the strength of the other. The movement of the sermon, like the movement of Christ in the world, is meant to lead from doubt to faith. We may begin by knocking on God's door, unsure whether anyone is now or has ever been at home, but when the door opens and we are led inside, doubt becomes moot. Our host takes it from us and hangs it in the closet with the dustpan and galoshes.

When the door opens in a sermon, it is because God has consented to be present. Sometimes it happens and sometimes it doesn't. When it does, there is no mistaking it. Fresh air pours into a stale room. Light crowds out all shadows. When it doesn't, that may have as much to do with our own failure to be present as with God's. Some preachers will pound away at a sermon without ever finding the handle to it, and some congregations will sit and stare at an open door without ever walking through it, but even our incompetence cannot shut God out for long. The living word of God is more able than we are. If we will remain with it, it will heal us, because God is in it.

Every preacher has a different routine for preparing a sermon. My own begins with a long sitting spell with an open Bible on my lap, as I read and read and read the text. What I am hunting for is the God in it, God for me and for my congregation at this particular moment in time. I am waiting to be addressed by the text by my own name, to be called out by it so that I look back at my human situation and see it from a new perspective, one that is more like God's. I am hoping for a moment of revelation I can share with those who will listen to me and I am jittery, because I never know what it may show me. I am not in control of the process. It is a process of discovery, in which I run the charged rod of God's word over the body of my own experience and wait to see where the sparks will fly. Sometimes the live current is harder to find than others but I keep at it, knowing that if there is no electricity for me, there will be none for the congregation either.

This means that I never know ahead of time what I will preach. If I did, then my sermons would be little more than lessons, expositions of things I already know that I think my listeners ought to know too. While there are preachers who do this sort of thing well, I am not one of them. I do not want to scatter pearls of wisdom from the pulpit; I want to discover something fresh—even if I cannot quite identify it yet, even if it is still covered with twigs and mud. I want to haul it into the pulpit and show others what God has shown me, while I am still shaking with excitement and delight.

The process of discovery begins with the text. Whether I like it or not, I approach it believing that God is in it and I commence the long, careful discipline of panning for gold. There are translations to be compared, words to be studied and puzzles to be solved. What is corban? How much is a talent? Where was Emmaus? More important, what did this passage mean to the one who first wrote it down? I am not free to pluck it out and use it in my own design. It has its own integrity. It is part of someone else's design, and the respectful preacher will work to discern its original meaning before imposing any other on it.

This is one of the hardest and most rewarding aspects of the job. We do not make sermons out of air: our creations, poor or brilliant as they may be, are always variations on someone else's theme. The main melody is always a given, and even when we launch into our own bold improvisations we are limited to a scale of eight notes. Our words are not ends in themselves; they exist to serve other words, which means that we never work alone. Sitting all by ourselves in our rooms with bitten pencils in our hands, we compose our sermons in partnership with all those who have done so before us. Together we explore the parameters of our common faith, testing the truth of one another's discoveries and holding each other accountable so that what we offer those who listen to us will not aim to dazzle but to nourish them.

Once I have done all my homework and have a decent idea what the text means, I give it a rest. Understanding is not enough. I do not want to pass on knowledge from the pulpit; I want to take part in an experience of God's living word, and that calls for a different kind of research. It is time to tuck the text into the pocket of my heart and walk around with it inside of me. It is time to turn its words and images loose on the events of my everyday life and see how they mix. It is time to daydream, whittle, whistle, pray. This is the gestation period of a sermon, and it cannot be rushed. It is a time of patient and impatient waiting for the stirring of the Holy Spirit, that bright bird upon whose brooding the sermon depends. Over and over again I check the nest of my notes and outlines, searching through them for some sign of life. I scan the text one more time and all of a sudden there is an egg in plain view, something where there had been nothing just a moment before, and the sermon is born.

What the egg contains is a connection, a likeness, between the life of the text and the life of the world. Sometimes it seems a brand new one, like the connection between Holy Communion and an infant's nursing, but more often it is an ancient one that suddenly catches the light. "God is love" (1 John 4:8). What could be more elementary? Everyone understands that; it is so simple that people put it on their car bumpers, right next to "Have a nice day." A preacher might explain that it means God is kindly disposed toward us, and that would be correct. But if, in the process of composing a sermon, a preacher discovers the visceral connection between the word "God" and the heart-pounding experience of authentic love, then the sermon will be more than correct. It will be true, not at the level of explanation but at the level of experience, where all our deepest truths are tested.

This is where a sermon becomes art. It is not enough to tell a congregation what they need to know about God, or Scripture, or life. The preacher who delivers airtight conclusions from the pulpit leaves the congregation with only two choices: they may agree with what they have heard or they may not, but they are prevented from drawing their own conclusions. The preacher has judged them incapable of that hard work and has done it for them. So when the sermon is over, it is over, unless they wish to praise or reject it as they shake hands at the door.

There is another way to preach, in which the preacher addresses the congregation not as mute students but as active partners in the process of discovering God's word. The sermon traces the preacher's own process of discovery, inviting the congregation to come along and providing them with everything they need to make their own finds. The movement of the sermon leads them past new vantage points on their common experience, so that they look at old landmarks from new perspectives. At each stop, the preacher pauses, pointing in a certain direction without telling the congregation what they should see when they look. It is up to them to discern what the landscape holds. The preacher's job is not to make the trip for them or to block their view, but to take them to the spot where they may best see for themselves. With any luck, where the sermon finally leads both preacher and congregation is into the presence of God, a place that cannot be explained but only experienced. When a sermon like this is over, it is not over. Everyone involved in it goes away with images, thoughts, and emotions that change and grow as the process of discovery goes on and on and on.

It is as hard for a preacher to say how this is done as it is for a painter to say how a tree takes shape on a canvas. Do the leaves come first or the branches? What combination of yellow and blue makes such a bright green? How do you make it look so real? All the parts of preaching can be taught: exegesis, language, metaphor, development, delivery. What is hard to teach is how to put them all together, so that what is true is also beautiful, and evocative, and alive. Life itself is the best teacher. Preachers who are attuned to God's presence and movement in the world do not have to invent much. All we have to learn is how to say what we see. We are not abstract artists, after all. We are God's impressionists, whose sermons reveal our hearts and minds as clearly as fingerprints. Every word choice, every illustration, every question our sermons ask tells the congregation who we are, but our self-disclosure goes even further than that.

"You are a word about the Word before you ever speak a word," Alan Jones said once. Everything we have ever done and everything we have become follows us into the pulpit when we preach. The way we stand there, the way we hold ourselves, what we do with our hands, where we focus our eyes—all of these preach sermons of their own, whatever we happen to be saying with our mouths. This makes preaching a form of prayer for me, an act of conscious self-offering in which I stand exposed before God and my neighbor, seeking relationship with them both. "Do you still get nervous?" a teenager asks me. Is the world still round? But my nervousness has less to do with performance anxiety than it does with standing so close to the truth of who I am before God. The success or failure of any particular sermon seems less important to me than the ongoing process of placing myself in God's hands.

The worst sermon I ever preached was in Canajoharie, New York, chewing gum capital of the world, where I was invited to address what was described to me as an ailing congregation. The gospel lesson for that Trinity Sunday was John's story about Nicodemus' search for new birth. It was a promising sign, I thought, and proceeded to construct an eight-page masterpiece on faith and doubt. Sunday morning arrived, the processional hymn began, and I marched into a church with three people in it—five, including me and my host. Two of them were elderly women, still weepy over the loss of a friend the day before. The third was a heavy, angry-looking man who occupied the other side of the church all by himself. Time came for the sermon and I crept into the pulpit, wondering what in the world to do. I tried the first page of my manuscript and abandoned it; it was like reciting poetry to a wall. With a fast prayer to the Holy Spirit for guidance, I put my notes away and tried to summarize what I had planned to say without them. The result was five minutes of pure gibberish. The Holy Spirit never showed up, and as my congregation stared blankly up at me I rapidly confirmed all their worst fears about women preachers.

One of the best sermons I ever preached was at the funeral of a baby girl. Her death, which came just three months after her complicated birth, tried the faith of everyone who knew her and her parents, including me. I worked and worked at something to say, but everywhere I turned I ran into the dead end of my own grief. Finally it came time to do the service and I walked into a full church with nothing but half a page of notes. When it was my turn to speak, I stood plucking the words out of thin air as they appeared before my eyes. Somehow, they worked. God consented to be present in them. But when I received a transcript of the sermon later from someone who had recorded the service, it was as if it had been written in disappearing ink. There was nothing there but a jumble of phrases and images, trailing off at the end into awkward silence. While the Holy Spirit was in them, they lived. Afterward, they were no more than empty boxes, lying where the wind had left them.

These two experiences remind me not to take myself too seriously. They also make me reluctant to talk about "best" and "worst" sermons. Something happens between the preacher's lips and the congregations' ears that is beyond prediction or explanation. The same sermon sounds entirely different at 9:00 and 11:15 A.M. on a Sunday morning. Sermons that make me weep leave my listeners baffled, and sermons that seem cold to me find warm responses. Later in the week, someone quotes part of my sermon back to me, something she has found extremely meaningful—only I never said it.

There is more going on here than anyone can say. Preaching is finally more than art or science. It is alchemy, in which tin becomes gold and yard rocks become diamonds under the influence of the Holy Spirit. It is a process of transformation for both preacher and congregation alike, as the ordinary details of their everyday lives are translated into the extraordinary elements of God's ongoing creation. When the drum roll begins and the preacher steps into place, we can count on that. Wherever God's word is, God is—loosening our tongues, tuning our ears, thawing our hearts—making us a people who may speak and hear the Word of Life.

Part Two

The Preaching of the Word

One Step at a Time

When they came to the house of the leader of the syna-
gogue, he saw a commotion, people weeping and wailing
loudly. When he had entered, he said to them, "Why do
you make a commotion and weep? The child is not dead
but sleeping." Mark 5:38-39

৵

It takes a lot of courage to be a human being. I have been holding a new goddaughter this week, and she does not know that yet. Just seven weeks old, she has eyes the color of the ocean. Looking into them, it is easy to see that she does not know anything about arthritis or thunderstorms or depression. She does not lie awake at night worrying about her relationships, or her job, or her death. There is no fear in those sea-blue eyes. She sleeps and eats and sighs when she is full. Her world is as wide as her mother's arms, and as safe. That is all she knows.

As my goddaughter ages, she will learn more. She will learn that bees sting and roses have thorns and that other children push and throw rocks. She will learn that having a fever is like being set on fire and that when your parents decide to move to another state, there is absolutely nothing you can do about it. All of that is part of growing up. It is not the only part, by a long shot, but it is the hard part, and it is part of how we learn what it is to be a human being.

Year after year, we add to our experience of the world, pushing against our limits to find out what will budge and what will not, and gradually we gain a sense of our own power. We find that we can make certain things happen and we can prevent other things from happening; we can make friends and we can make enemies; we can say yes, and we can say no.

Some of us get so carried away with this discovery that we begin to think we are in control of our lives. We come of age and we decide what to be. We open bank accounts and make five-year plans. We take our vitamins and work out three times a week at the gym. We space our children two years apart and raise them by the book, and nine-tenths of the time it actually seems to work, enough of the time so that we convince ourselves it is true: that if you just do everything right, then everything will turn out all right, that human beings really can take charge of their lives.

Until something happens. The income evaporates, the doctor finds a spot on the X ray, the child's grades go down and down, and it is like being trapped inside a fine automobile when the brakes fail. In a split second everything changes. One moment you are comfortably and safely in command of your journey, and the next you are being flung down the road in an expensive piece of machinery that will not stop.

"I've lost control!" That is what good people say when bad things happen to them. "I've lost control of my life!" I have said it myself, but it is not true. Human beings do not lose control of their lives. What we lose is the illusion that we were ever in control of our lives in the first place, and it is a hard, hard lesson to learn—so hard that most of us have to go back to the blackboard again and again, because we keep thinking that there must be some way to work it out, some way to master the human condition so that there are no leaks in it, no scares, no black holes.

As far as I know, it cannot be done. Maybe that is why it is called the human *condition*. Like asthma or myopia, being human is a condition we live with—a splendid one in most respects—but one with certain built-in limitations. Some things will budge for us and some will not. We cannot fly. We cannot live forever. We cannot control everything that happens to us. That is the human condition, and it can be frightening, because what that means is we cannot choose all the circumstances of our lives. All we can really choose is how we respond to them, and that is why it takes a lot of courage to be a human being.

The Bible is full of this. Jesus and his disciples are out on the lake when a heavy storm blows up. Eight-foot waves swamp the boat, lightning pops overhead with a sound like a bullwhip. The disciples are terrified. The wind and the sea are beyond their control, while Jesus lies sleeping on a pillow in the stern.

"Teacher," they cry, "do you not care that we are perishing?" Waking up, Jesus says, "Peace! Be still!" and the squall stops just like that. "Why are you afraid?" he asks them. "Have you still no faith?" (Mark 4:35-40).

A man possessed by an unclean spirit lives in a Gerasene graveyard. No one can control him. His ankles are scarred from the fetters he has snapped in two. Everyone is afraid of him until Jesus shows up. "Come out of the man," he says to the unclean spirit, and the man's sanity is restored (Mark 5:1-15).

Or take this story, which follows on the heels of these other two in Mark's gospel. Jesus crosses the lake again and has not been on shore five minutes when one of the leaders of the synagogue, Jairus by name, falls at his feet. He too is suffering from the human condition; he too is up against something he cannot control—not a storm this time, or an unclean spirit, but a threat against the life of his child. His little girl is close to death and there is nothing he can do, nothing but lie in the dirt and beg: "Come and lay your hands on her," he beseeches Jesus, "so that she may be made well, and live."

But before Jesus can follow him home, the worst possible news comes. It is too late; she is gone. Only Jesus ignores this version of the truth. Turning to Jairus, he delivers the shortest sermon of his career: "Do not fear," he says to the grief-besotted man, "only believe."

It is not just a word for Jairus; it is a word for all of us who suffer from the human condition, who are up against things we cannot control. Only believe what? That our prayers will be answered? That things will turn out the way we think they should? That we will get what we want? That is the way it seems to work in the stories. People call on Jesus and they get what they want. The storm stops, the demon departs, the little girl gets up and walks around. So naturally we try to figure out what those people did right so that we can do it too, so that the same thing will happen to us.

Only that is not what the stories are about. They are not stories about how to get God to do what we want, which is just another way of trying to stay in control. Instead, they are stories about who God is, and how God acts, and what God is like. Mark wrote them down for one reason and one reason alone: "This is no ordinary man," he tells us every way he knows how. "This man is the son of God. Believe it."

Mark wanted people to believe that so they would have strength to meet the days to come. He wanted them to believe that Jesus was who he said he was so that later, after he was gone, they would not lose heart. He wanted them to believe that even when he was not around to talk with them face to face anymore, that he still had the power to calm their storms and send their demons away and restore them to life in new and different ways.

New and different because his own death changed everything, by its very ordinariness. He was nailed to a cross, he bled and he died, in very short order. Those who came expecting mighty acts from him went away disappointed, because there at the end he was up against the human condition just like the rest of us. That is what he consented to do, so that God could show us the possibilities: how one human being, willing to lose control of his life, might receive it back again—not for a time, but for all time, and for all humankind as well.

"Do not fear," he says, "only believe." Only believe what? He does not say, but those are the two choices, apparently, when human beings discover that they are not in charge after all. They can fear, or they can believe. They can panic and fall overboard or they can ride out the storm. They can despair or they can wait, very quietly, for sanity to return. They can be afraid or they can believe. Judging by my own experience, it is almost never a matter of either/or. I do not know anyone who believes all the time, but I do know how both fear and belief feel, and that there is a palpable difference between the two.

Fear is a small cell with no air in it and no light. It is suffocating inside, and dark. There is no room to turn around inside it. You can only face in one direction, but it hardly matters since you cannot see anyhow. There is no future in the dark. Everything is over. Everything is past. When you are locked up like that, tomorrow is as far away as the moon.

People can stop by and tap on your walls. They can even bang on the door to show you where it is, but when you are afraid you cannot open up. They might not be who they say they are. They might just make things worse. It is safer to stay where you are, where you know what is what, even if you cannot breathe, even if you cannot move. That is how fear feels.

Belief is something else altogether, although it is not what some would have us believe. It is not a well-fluffed nest, or a well-defended castle high on a hill. It is more like a rope bridge over a scenic gorge, sturdy but swinging back and forth, with plenty of light and plenty of air but precious little to hang on to except the stories you have heard: that it is the best and only way across, that it is possible, that it will bear your weight.

All you have to do is believe in the bridge more than you believe in the gorge, but fortunately you do not have to believe in it all by yourself. There are others to believe it with you, and even some to believe it for you when your own belief wears thin. They have crossed the bridge ahead of you and are waiting on the other side. You can talk to them if you like, as you step into the air, putting one foot ahead of the other, just that: just one step at a time.

It takes a lot of courage to be a human being, but if Jesus was who he said he was, the bridge will hold. Believing in him will not put us in charge, or get us what we want or even save us from all harm, but believing in him, we may gradually lose our fear of our lives. Whatever the human condition we find ourselves in, we may finally learn to live it, maybe even to love it, if only because we believe he lives and loves it too.

The Fourth Watch

He came towards them early in the morning, walking on the sea. He intended to pass them by. But when they saw him walking on the sea, they thought it was a ghost and cried out; for they all saw him and were terrified. But immediately he spoke to them and said, "Take heart, it is I; do not be afraid." Mark 6:48-50

ঽ৯

It is hard to tell exactly what happened that dark, windy night. Mark's account is one of three different versions in the Bible. Luke skips the story of Jesus walking on the water altogether, while John offers the Cliff Notes version: the sea was rough, the disciples were scared, Jesus spoke, and before they could haul him aboard, the boat immediately arrived at the far shore. No ghost, no ceasing of the wind, no astonishment.

I suppose Matthew's account is the best known, with Peter's brave but failed attempt to meet Jesus out on the waves, followed by Jesus' quick rebuke—"You of little faith, why did you doubt?"—after which the wind dropped and the disciples did too. One by one they fell to their knees in the bottom of the boat and there among the dried bait and tangled nets, they confessed their faith. "Truly," they said, "you are the Son of God" (Matt. 14:28-33).

Mark is not so kind to the disciples, nor to us his listeners. His account of Jesus' walk across the water is a more disturbing one, full of puzzling details that come to a gloomy end. Jesus makes his disciples get into their boat after the feeding of the five thousand, Mark tells us, which means they push off from the shore close to dark. But who sails at night who does not have to? Then he tells us that they are headed to the other side, to Bethsaida, which poses another problem, since Bethsaida is not on the other side at all but far to the north.

Then comes the wind, so strong that the disciples row in place half the night before Jesus comes to them—but not really to them, as it turns out. He means to pass them by (did you notice that line in the story?), but they mistake him for a ghost and yell out loud with fright, which gets his attention. So he stops to reassure them, climbs into the boat with them and the wind stops, just like that, for which they do not even say thank you because they are too astounded. They know who he is, you see, but they still do not know who he is.

Now for me, at least, this is not a satisfying story. I prefer a little more bravado in my disciples, or at least the assurance that they have learned their lesson. But according to Mark they just did not get it. They did not recognize that their rabbi was also the Messiah they had been waiting for, and it was not very satisfying for Mark either. The only explanation he could think of was that their hearts were hardened—their minds were closed—so that they did not understand the miracle of the loaves or much of anything else, for that matter.

Maybe that explains why they were not glad to see Jesus. Never mind for a moment that he meant to pass them by—they did not know that, so why weren't they overjoyed to see him? Why didn't they welcome being rescued from the storm and help him into the boat with loud sounds of relief? Well, in the first place, it was not the storm they were afraid of. The rowing may have been raising some blisters on their hands, but they were not afraid of anything, as far as we can tell. According to Mark, they did not feel or say anything at all until they saw a figure approaching them across the water—*on top of the water*—at which point they cried out and were terrified.

They were, I say, fine until they saw a ghost. It would probably have been fine with them to row all night, if that is what it took to get where they were going. They were not schoolteachers or poets, after all—they were fishermen, most of them, bluecollar workers who were used to hard labor. They did not mind pitting themselves against the elements, gutting it out, doing whatever it took to get the job done. As disciples went, they were high achievers. They could be counted on to produce, at least as long as no one messed with them. So the storm was not the problem; Jesus was, and he continued to be even after he had soothed them, and identified himself, and made the wind stop. When he did *that*, his disciples were utterly astounded—not by the waves, mind you, but by the calm. They did not understand, Mark says, because their hearts were hardened.

I do not know many fishermen, but I do know a few sailors, who are some of the nicest people you would ever want to meet but who are also some of the most—well, you could call them superstitious or you could just say how *respectful* they are of what can happen to you in a boat on the sea in the middle of the night. When I asked one of them what time it was that the fourth watch rolled around—which was when Jesus came to his disciples—his eyes got big.

"Oh," he said, "that's the watch just before dawn, when the funny stuff starts to happen. Everyone else is asleep and it's just you out there surrounded by black water as far as you can see—especially if there's no moon—and your eyes start to play tricks on you. You stare at the waves long enough and you begin to think you see land, or worse. You think you see rocks rising right up in front of you, or phantom ships drifting with all their lights off, or sea monsters.

"Pretty soon the waves start sounding like people whispering, or like the breathing of some huge invisible being.

97

Then you start realizing just how alone you are, and how far from home, and how many ways there are for you to die. But you can't think about that too long or you'll go crazy, so you make a peanut butter sandwich, or see how many hymns you can whistle, or polish the compass until the sun comes up."

Or in the words of Mark's gospel, you row and row and row. You stay busy. You stay focused on the far shore, on your destination, and you dismiss everything that gets in your way.

The disciples' hearts were hardened, Mark says. They had cardiosclerosis: that part of them most capable of feeling, of understanding, of encountering God was clogged up so that very little could get through to them anymore. Their hearts were all but shut down and they did not even know it. Maybe it was stress: all that hard work, hammering away at the parables, preaching repentance, anointing the sick, casting out demons, trying to put something—anything—into all those damp hands that reached out to them for food, for health, for love. Or maybe it was their diet: eating on the run wherever their work carried them, moving from place to place, roast lamb one night and a few dried fish the next. Or maybe it was God, casting a shadow over their hearts for God's own inscrutable reasons.

Whatever the reason, they had heart conditions. They were handicapped, and they used what they had left to survive as best they could, to try harder, to row and row and row. It was what they were called to do, and they were prepared to do it all night if necessary. What they were *not* prepared to do was to see their Lord hiking toward them across the Sea of Galilee—unsummoned, traveling in a most unorthodox manner in the middle of the night. It did not fit their expectations; it violated all their categories. He could not have surprised them more if he had come to them as an arthritic old man with sour breath, or a smooth-talking saleswoman with an alligator briefcase, or an obviously disturbed stranger asking directions around town.

He was not supposed to be there at all, and so they did not see him. They saw a ghost instead, which was all they *could* see with what was left of their hearts. Intent on their duties, on guard against all the things that go bump in the night, they mistook their Lord for a spook, for someone who meant to do them harm, but he did not hold it against them. He may have meant to pass them by, but when in their fear they cried out, immediately he stopped to comfort them. "Take heart," he said, he who had such a surplus of heart to offer them. "Take heart, it is I; do not be afraid." And the wind ceased, and they were utterly astounded, for they did not understand about the loaves or the wind or anything. Their hearts were hardened, but he got into the boat with them anyway. Their hearts made it difficult for them to accept him, so he accepted them instead.

After that, things got easier right away. There was no more wind, no rowing, just some easy paddling, which gave them lots of time to talk, and rub their sore muscles, and laugh about what an unusual day it had been all the way around. I do not know if their hearts got any softer, then or ever. According to Mark, Jesus had harsh words for his disciples at least twice again, berating them for their stubbornness, for their dullness, for having eyes that did not see and ears that did not hear, but none of that ever seemed to interrupt his love for them.

They remained his chosen people, clogged hearts and all, and he remained their Lord—not only the Lord of the sea but also the Lord of the land and of the whole creation—who kept climbing into their boats to be with them over and over again from that day forth forevermore, with heart enough to spare, oh with heart enough for us all.

I Am Who I Am

They said to him, "Who are you?" Jesus said to them, "Why do I speak to you at all?" John 8:25

℀

The eighth chapter of John does not do much for me. I like stories, not speeches. I like a passage with a plot, with characters, with a beginning and an end. I like something you can get hold of—something with boats in it, or bread, or birds of the air. But the Bible does not always give me what I like, and what it has given me this time is a really mean-spirited debate between Jesus and the Pharisees in the temple at Jerusalem.

For two whole pages they call each other names, and question each other's sanity and dispute each other's parentage. It is not pleasant, and it is not even very clear. Most of it sounds like a course in advanced metaphysics, but I decided to stick with it because I believe that God never wastes my time or yours either. Whether we like what we get or whether we do not, God has promised to be present to us in it, and that is as true in life as it is in Scripture.

Our tendency is to pick and choose—to reject the parts of life we do not like and keep shopping for some we do. When God's gifts come wrapped in shiny paper and curled ribbons, we say, "Thank you very much," but when they arrive on our doorsteps held together with newspaper and barbed wire, most of us take out our magic markers and write "Return to Sender" on the box. But there is another way open to us. We can accept what we have been assigned and work with it—taking it apart piece by piece, if necessary, in order to discover the God inside.

What we have been assigned today is one more episode in Jesus' long controversy with the Pharisees about who he is. From our safe distance, it is easy to simplify any story with Pharisees in it by making them the bad guys, but they are just doing their job. They are the defenders of the faith; they are the religious authorities in charge of keeping holy things holy, and they do not like Jesus' type—especially the way John's gospel presents him. In John's gospel, Jesus says "I" a lot—I, I, I—"I am the bread of life" (6:35), "I am the good shepherd" (10:11), "I am the true vine" (15:1), "I am the way, and the truth, and the life. No one comes to the Father, except through me" (14:6).

Those are fairly outrageous claims for anyone to make, but for a Hebrew they are really unthinkable. For a Hebrew there is only *one* good shepherd, *one* true vine, *one* bread of life, and that is almighty God. Who does Jesus think he is? That is what the Pharisees want to know. He passes himself off as a believer in God, but that is not how he sounds. He sounds like a rival, one of those dangerously attractive preachers who get carried away by their own charisma and get the message all confused with the messenger.

"I am the light of the world." That is the last thing Jesus said, the remark that brought the Pharisees charging after him like bulls to a red flag. But when they challenge him, things get worse, not better. "You are from below," Jesus tells them. "I am from above; you are of this world, I am not of this world...you will die in your sins unless you believe that I am he."

"Unless you believe that I am he." That is the way it reads in English, but in Greek there is no "he" on the end: "Unless you believe that I am." That is what Jesus really says, and it drives the Pharisees wild. They hear what he is up to; they hear the echo that he means them to hear. "I am," he says, and any Hebrew worth his salt remembers another voice that said, "I am who I am."

It was the voice of almighty God, addressing Moses from the burning bush, making him the first human being on earth to know the name of God. "Thus you shall say to the Israelites," God instructed him, "I AM has sent me to you" (Exod. 3:14). "I AM." The name of God. "You will die in your sins unless you believe that I am."

Can you see why the Pharisees get upset? Jesus is using God's name—*abusing* it, as far as they are concerned—but when they try to show him the error of his ways, he tells them *they* are the ones who are wrong, and if they do not believe he is who he says he is, then they will die in their sins. "Who are you?" they ask him, and you can almost hear the exasperation in their voices, but you can hear it in Jesus' reply as well: "Why do I speak to you at all?"

He does not answer the question. Did you notice that? "Who are you?" hangs in the air, and for many of us it hangs there still, *the* question of the faith, the one question we ought to know the answer to and the one question that continues to haunt many of us because we do *not* know the answer, not completely, not in any way that is easy to say. "Who are you?" That is the question. Who is Jesus, and who is he to us, and what does our answer to that question have to do with our eternal lives?

I am not talking about proper names, by the way. We have plenty of those. He is the Messiah, the Lamb of God, the second person of the Trinity, the Savior of the world. But knowing someone's name is not the same thing as knowing that person. If you do not believe me, then try it on a three year old.

"Who is Jesus?" she asks, riding home from church with her Sunday school picture in her hand: a tall thin man in a blue robe, with sheep around his legs and a lamb in his arms.

"He is the son of God," you say, with great authority.

"I know that," she says, "but who *is* he?"

"The redeemer of the world?" you say. "The Lord, the giver of life."

"I thought that was God," she says.

"Jesus is God too," you say.

"Then how can he be the son of God?" she asks.

"That is a very good question," you say, and offer to buy her a frozen yogurt for being such a smart little girl, but you have not answered her question and it hangs there between you, the question you both want the answer to: "Jesus, who are you?"

One afternoon when I was a sophomore in college I was sitting in my dormitory room minding my own business when someone knocked on the door. I opened it and found two young women clutching Bibles to their breasts. My heart sank. With my parents' help, I had avoided organized religion most of my life, and these two—with their gleaming eyes, their earnest faces, their modest plaid skirts and sensible shoes—these were just the sort of people I had hoped to continue avoiding as long as I could. The Holy Spirit had sent them, they said. Could they come in? While I was thinking of a suitable reply, they did come in, and I was a goner. They sat down on my bed, opened their Bibles, and began to ask me questions.

"Are you saved?" one of them asked.

"Well," I said, "that depends on what you—"

"No," the other one said, writing something down on a pad of paper.

"Do you want to be saved?" the first one asked, and both of them gleamed at me while I thought how awful it would sound to say, "No."

"Sure," I said, and they leapt into action, pulling me down to sit beside them on the bed, one of them reading selected passages of Scripture while the other one drew an illustration of my predicament on her pad.

"Here you are," she said, drawing a stick figure on one side of a yawning chasm. "And here is God," she said, drawing another figure on the other side. "In between is sin and death," she said, filling the chasm with dark clouds from her pen.

"Now the question is, how are you and God going to get together?" she asked me.

"I don't have a clue," I said, and they both looked delighted. Then the one with the pen bent over her drawing and connected the two sides of the chasm with a bridge in the shape of a cross.

"That's how," she said. "Jesus laid down his life for you to cross over. Do you want to cross over?"

"Sure," I said, and the look in their eyes was like one of those old cash registers where you crank the handle and the little "Sale" sign pops up. They told me to kneel by my bed, where they knelt on either side of me and instructed me to repeat after them: "I accept Jesus Christ as my personal Lord and Savior and I ask him to come into my life. Amen." Then they got up, hugged me, gave me a schedule of campus Bible study, and left.

The whole thing took less than twenty minutes. It was quick, simple, direct. *They* did not have any questions about who Jesus was. You are here, God is there, Jesus is the bridge. Say these words and you are a Christian. Abracadabra. Amen. It is still hard for me to describe my frame of mind at the time. I was half-serious, half-amused. I cooperated as much out of curiosity as anything, and because I thought that going along with them would get them out of my room faster than arguing with them.

I admired their courage, in a way, but nothing they said really affected me. Most of it was just embarrassing, the kind of simplistic faith I liked the least, but something happened to me that afternoon. After they left I went out for a walk and the world looked funny to me, different. People's faces looked different to me; I had never noticed so many details before. I stared at them like portraits in a gallery, and my own face burned for over an hour. Meanwhile, it was hard to walk. The ground was spongy under my feet. I felt weightless, and it was all I could do to keep myself from floating up and getting stuck in the trees.

Was it a conversion? All I know is that something happened, something that got my attention and has kept it through all the years that have passed since then. I may have been fooling around, but Jesus was not. My heart may not have been in it, but Jesus' was. I asked him to come in and he came in, although I no more have words for his presence in my life than I do for what keeps the stars in the sky or what makes the daffodils rise up out of their graves each spring. It just is. He just is. "Who are you?" "I am."

That is the answer the Pharisees could not accept because they could not see through it. It was opaque for them, a claim that caused terrible problems for them no matter how they looked at it. Whether Jesus was speaking *for* God or *instead* of God, he was way, way out of line, claiming equality with a God who had no equals. The way they saw it, there was only one great I AM and Jesus was not it.

But there is another way to view his answer—not as opaque but transparent—the answer of someone who does not claim equality with God, but intimacy, whose being is so wrapped up in the being of God that when he says, "I am," there is no difference between the two. When you look at him, you see God. When you listen to him, you hear God. Not because he has taken God's place, but because he is the clear window God has glazed into flesh and blood—the porthole between this world and the next, the passageway between heaven and earth.

"When you have lifted up the Son of Man, then you will realize that I am he," he tells his critics. He is speaking, of course, about his own death. When that has come to pass, then they will be able to see through him. Then they will know what his "I am" means—that he claims nothing for himself, not even his own life; that he does nothing under his own authority. The only reason he *is* at all is to reveal the "I am" of his father and to bring others into intimate relationship with the Chief Being of the universe.

"Then you will realize," he said, but he was wrong. They lifted him up and still they did not realize who he was, just as we lift him up in the broken bread of communion and wonder ourselves. "Who are you?" That is the question that hangs in the air, drawing us deeper and deeper into the mystery. We realize who he is, but who is he, really? He has come into our lives and rearranged our worlds and made our faces burn with his brightness, but who is he and why can't we be more articulate about who he is?

One reason, perhaps, is that the answer is not ours to give. "Who are you?" is a question addressed not to us, but to Jesus, and one that he does not, on this particular day, answer. He has answered before and he will answer again, but it is rarely the same answer. "I am the bread, the shepherd, the vine, the light; I am the way, the truth, the life." Which is it? All of the above? Or none of them? God, or son of God? My personal Lord and Savior, or the cosmic Christ?

We cannot nail him down. We tried once, but he got loose, and ever since then he has been the walking, talking presence of God in our midst, the living presence of God in our lives. If we cannot say who he is in twenty-five words or less, it is because he is our window on the undefinable, unfathomable I AM, and we cannot sum him up any easier than we can sum up the one who sent him.

"Who are you?" That is the only question worth asking.

"I am." That is the only answer we need.

The Tenth Leper

As he entered a village, ten lepers approached him. Keeping their distance, they called out, saying, "Jesus, Master, have mercy on us!" When he saw them, he said to them, "Go and show yourselves to the priests." And as they went, they were made clean. Then one of them, when he saw that he was healed, turned back, praising God with a loud voice. He prostrated himself at Jesus' feet and thanked him. And he was a Samaritan. Then Jesus asked, "Were not ten made clean? But the other nine, where are they?" Luke 17:12-17

ॐ

L epers became part of my nightmare repertoire at an early age, after I went with my parents to a film directed by Federico Fellini. I don't remember what town we lived in then, or what the movie was about, but I do remember the lepers. They lived in caves, out of which they crept like vampires, shielding themselves from the light, their heads hooded, their whole bodies hidden under tattered shrouds. The first sound was the tinkle of the bells they wore around their necks, but as they approached the camera—as they approached me—they began to cry out in their tiny voices. "Unclean! Unclean!" they cried, as they stretched out their hands for food—hands missing thumbs, missing fingers, which was horrible enough, but then they were on top of me and I looked up into their hungry, eaten faces—faces that have been with me ever since.

That is, thank God, the extent of my acquaintance with lepers, but not so for the people of the Bible. Leprosy was a dread but common affliction in those days, so common, in fact, that lepers had a prescribed social role, and a religious one too. The book of Leviticus spends two whole chapters teaching priests how to diagnose diseases of the skin, how to pronounce lepers ritually unclean, how to perform rites of purification should they be healed. As for the lepers: The one "who has the disease shall wear torn clothes and let the hair of his head hang loose, and he shall cover his lip and cry, 'Unclean, unclean.' He shall remain unclean as long as he has the disease; he is unclean; he shall dwell alone in a habitation outside the camp" (Lev. 13:45-46).

Leprosy was not seen, however, as a punishment for sin. It was understood instead as an inexplicable act of God, which made it even more frightening. If there was nothing you did to deserve leprosy then it followed that there was nothing you could do to avoid it, and so lepers were shunned—because their disease was contagious, certainly, but it was more than that. It was their pain, their loneliness, their unspeakable fear no one wanted to catch, and so they were kept at a distance, barred from the religious community, and declared unworthy of God. They were the unclean outsiders, not to be mistaken as having anything in common with the healthy insiders. Understand? They live over there; we live over here. We are not like them. God knows we feel sorry for them, but you have got to be sensible about these things.

None of this was challenged by the lepers themselves. They could not work, after all, and they depended upon the charity of the insiders for their livelihood. So they dressed as they were told, and spoke as they were told, and did not cross over the line that had been drawn to separate them from those with unblemished skin. They were obedient. They followed their orders, and even when Jesus, that renowned healer of lepers, came to town they did not break rank. They stood at the proper distance and said the proper things. "Jesus, Master," they said, calling him by his messianic title, "have mercy upon us."

So he looked at them and saw what anyone could see, that they were eaten up with leprosy and needed all the mercy they could get. He did not touch them—there was no mud, no spittle, no talk of faith this time, just an order: "Go and show yourselves to the priests," Jesus said, and they did, disappearing as obediently as they had appeared in the first place.

None of them asked why, but there was only one reason to go see the priests and that was to receive a diagnosis, a verdict: clean or unclean, insider or out, member of the community or beggar on the outskirts of town. None of them asked why, but as they went to do as they were told they were cleansed—the scabs went away, the color returned, the feeling came back into limbs that had been numb for years. And nine went on to do as they were told, to have the priests in Jerusalem certify their cures and restore them to society.

But one did not do as he was told. One, when he saw that he was healed, cried out, turned back, and did not rest until he lay on his face in the dirt at Jesus' feet, praising God and giving thanks. He made a spectacle of himself, all the more so once he was recognized as a Samaritan, a believer in the Torah as far as he was concerned, but a Gentile and foreigner as far as the house of David was concerned. He was, in other words, a double outsider—once by virtue of his leprosy and twice by virtue of his non-Jewish blood—a double loser lying at the feet of Jesus and thanking God as if God were somehow present in a man, and somehow revealed in the presence of that man. He was one of the unclean who saw what the clean could not see, and who refused to be separated from what gave him life.

It is hard to say what effect the tenth leper's response had on Jesus. Something happened, because all of a sudden he started asking questions: "Weren't there ten lepers here a minute ago? Where are the other nine? Is this foreigner the only one who knows how to say thank you?" he said, and then turned to the tenth leper. "Rise and go your way," he said; "your faith has made you well." Or straight from the Greek, "Your faith has saved you."

Once you stop to think about it, this is all very odd. Didn't Jesus tell all ten to go show themselves to the priests? And didn't nine do what they were told? Didn't this one, in fact, not do what he was told, and even flaunt his disobedience with a great sloppy show of emotion? And weren't all ten healed? Then how come this one got special treatment, got told his faith had made him well? Weren't all ten made well? What is going on here?

Ten were healed of their skin diseases, but only one was saved. Ten were declared clean and restored to society, but only one was said to have faith. Ten set out for Jerusalem to claim their free gifts as they were told, but only one turned back and gave himself to the Giver instead. Ten behaved like good lepers, good Jews; only one, a double loser, behaved like a man in love. There is a lot going on here.

At this church we leave the sanctuary open five days a week from nine to five, like the banks and businesses that surround us. We like to think of it as a peace offering to our corporate neighbors. We keep it dim and cool inside, a kind of oasis in the middle of the city where passersby can stop and be quiet for a while, stop and look, stop and listen. But as you also know, the city is full of all kinds of people, and not everyone comes in here with godly intentions. So we have installed a closed circuit television camera to keep an eye on the place, to make sure no one runs off with the candlesticks or does anything unseemly in the pews, like drink or sleep or embrace. You have got to be sensible about these things.

The monitor sits beside the receptionist's desk in the parish office, where the volunteer on the desk can keep watch over the altar and its furnishings. One day last fall the receptionist on duty became concerned. "There's a man lying face down on the altar steps," she said. "I wouldn't bother you, but he's been there for hours. Every now and then he stands up, raises his arms toward the altar, and lies down again. Do you think he's all right?" Four priests and several staff members conferred over the matter and elected the parish superintendent to go check on the man. As he did so, we all huddled around the monitor to watch. Our envoy appeared on the screen, walked up to the man, exchanged a few words with him, and returned to the parish office.

"He says he's praying."

"Aha," we said, thanking him for this information.

It went on for days. Every morning around eleven the receptionist would look up from her desk and there he would be, prostrate before the altar, his hair in knots, his worn clothes covered with dustballs from the floor. The sexton cleaned around him; the altar guild tried not to disturb him when they came to polish the silver; the florist asked if he should leave the flowers somewhere else but we said no, just step over the man and put them on the altar where they belong.

We discussed the problem at staff meeting. "Should we do something?" someone asked. "I don't know," said someone else, "what do you think?"

"I think I want to get on that guy's prayer list," one of us said, and we all laughed.

Finally it was Sunday, and my turn to celebrate communion at the early service. He was there when I arrived, blocking my path to the altar, and I did not know what to do. Maybe he was drunk, surely he was crazy—what would happen if I asked him to move? Approaching him as if I were approaching a land mine, I tapped him on the shoulder. He was so skinny, so dirty. "Excuse me," I said, "but there's going to be a service in here in a few minutes. I'm sorry, but you'll have to move."

He lifted his forehead from the floor and spoke with a heavy Haitian accent. "That's okay," he said, rising and dusting himself off in one dignified motion. Then he left, and he never came back. The eight o'clock service began on

time. The faithful took their places and I took mine. We read
our parts well. We spoke when we were supposed to speak
and were silent when we were supposed to be silent. We offered up our symbolic gifts, we performed our bounden
duty and service, and there was nothing wrong with what
we did, nothing at all. We were good servants, careful and
contrite sinners who had come for our ritual cleansing, but
one of us was missing. The foreigner was no longer among
us; he had risen and gone his way, but the place where he
lay on his face for hours—making a spectacle of himself—
seemed all at once so full of heat and light that I stepped
around it on my way out, chastened if only for that moment
by the call to a love so excessive, so disturbing, so beyond
the call to obedience that it made me want to leave all my
good works behind.

But that was a long time ago now, and what has become
apparent in the meantime is that I know how to be obedient
but I do not know how to be in love. It does not seem to be
an ability I can command, like reflective listening or public
speaking. And so I do what I know how to do, and I do it as
well as I know how. I read my Bible, say my prayers, pay
my pledge. And there is nothing wrong with that, nothing at
all. It is that kind of steady, law-abiding discipleship—the
discipleship of the nine lepers—that has kept the great ship
of the church afloat for thousands of years. I am one of the
nine, but it is the tenth leper who interests me—the outsider,
the double loser, who captures my imagination—the one
whose disease I fear, whose passion confounds me, whom I
may not see at all because he does not need a priest to certify his cure.

"Where are the nine?" Jesus asks, but I know where they
are. "Where is the tenth leper?" That is what I want to know.
Where is the one who followed his heart instead of his instructions, who accepted his life as a gift and gave it back
again, whose thanksgiving rose up from somewhere so deep
inside him that it turned him around, changed his direction,
led him to Jesus, made him well? Where are the nine? Where
is the tenth? Where is the disorderly one who failed to go

along with the crowd, the impulsive one who fell on his face in the dirt, the fanatical one who loved God so much that obedience was beside the point? Where did that one go?

Not that I am likely to go after him. It is safer here with the nine—we know the rules and who does what. We are the ones upon whom the institution depends. But the missing one, the one who turned back, or was turned away, or turned against—where did he go? Who is he, and whom is he with, and what does he know that we do not know? Where are the nine? We are here, right here. But where, for the love of God, is the tenth?

Do Love

"Which of these three, do you think, was a neighbor to the man who fell into the hands of the robbers?" He said, "The one who showed him mercy." Jesus said to him, "Go and do likewise." Luke 10:36-37

❧

All things considered, I am a pretty good thinker. If people will be patient with me, I can understand almost anything but football and the stock market, and figuring things out gives me the same thrill I imagine a fly-fisherman must feel when he lands a big rainbow trout. I remember how once in seminary I spent four straight hours in the library with a ten-pound theology book by Karl Barth, reading and rereading his chapter on the dual natures of Christ, or something pithy like that, and failing utterly to understand what he was getting at. So I kept biting my fingernails and drinking black coffee until finally—on about the fifth time through—I got it, really got it, and I had to go outside to the quadrangle so I could scream.

While I no longer remember the content of my revelation, I do remember being surprised that the quadrangle had not changed because of it. The trees were right where they had always been, the red brick buildings looked exactly like they had before. Things may have been different because I understood, but only inside of me, and I was vaguely disappointed that the world had not benefited from my new knowledge.

I feel the same excitement about the spoken word. The hair stands up on my arms when I hear something said well or say it well myself, and of course that makes me love the art of preaching. When I hear someone take a biblical text apart, wake up the tired language and set the trapped images free, then put that same text back together again so that it positively gleams with new meaning, I have to go outside and scream. But lo and behold, when I get there—bursting at the seams with my new understanding—everything looks just the same as it did before. The most perfect sermon in the world is still an exercise in talking, and hearing, and understanding, but apparently the world could care less unless somehow or another it is translated into action.

Take this sermon, for instance. I have been thinking all week about the parable of the Good Samaritan, reading creative commentaries on it and talking it over with my friends. At least one of the truths I got from it was that God comes to us daily in unexpected encounters with unexpected people, and if we are on the ball, we will not ignore them. Then Thursday I was driving to work through the early morning drizzle, my seat belt on and my doors locked, when I saw a car with its hood up on Howell Mill Road. As I approached, a tall black man stepped into the road, holding up a pair of jumper cables and looking me straight in the eye. Several hundred pieces of information went through my mind in about three seconds. "The man needs help—you are a single woman alone in a car—the man needs help—never open your door to a stranger—go to the nearest service station and send a mechanic—the man needs help—what if he cannot afford a mechanic?—the man needs help—I am sorry, I cannot help—maybe the next person will." And I drove on to work, to complete my research on the Good Samaritan.

So that is why I do not want to talk about him this morning. You already know his story, anyway. He is the guy in the black hat who turns out to be the hero; he is the heretical outcast who is a better Jew than the Jews. He is the redneck in overalls with Gilmer County plates on his truck who stops for the guy on Howell Mill and not only jumps his car but buys him a new battery as well, leaving fifty dollars with the mechanic at the Goodyear Store to fix anything else that might be wrong. I do not understand him. The person I do understand is the lawyer, the character in today's story who inspired Jesus to tell the story of the Good Samaritan in the first place.

He is, above all, a smart person, with a well-trained mind. He is logical but also imaginative; he can make connections between seemingly unrelated facts and still root out the inconsistencies when other people try to do the same thing. He is concerned with the law, if not with justice, and with drawing the line between right and wrong. Finally, because he is following Jesus around, the lawyer in this morning's story is also a person who is hungry for God, and who wishes to know what the life of faith might require of him.

"What must I do to inherit eternal life?" he asks Jesus, and who does not wonder that? Who does not want that? Life with no end, life with no death. For some people, eternal life means heaven, the jackpot at the end of the rainbow, but to hear Jesus talk about it, eternal life also means hitting the jackpot *now*; eternal life means enjoying a depth and breadth and sweetness of life that is available right this minute and not only after we have breathed our last. But even if you believe that, how do you get it? What must you do to experience it? That is the question put to Jesus by the lawyer. "Teacher," he says, "what must I do to inherit eternal life?"

In good rabbinical fashion, Jesus does not answer him. The lawyer wants someone else to hand him the key. He wants the answer to come from outside himself, but Jesus wants him to discover it for himself and so he answers his question with a question. "What is written in the law?" he asks the man. "What do you read there?" The lawyer answers him beautifully.

"You shall love the Lord your God with all your heart, and with all your soul, and with all your strength, and with all your mind; and your neighbor as yourself." It is one of those answers that makes the hair stand up on your arms. It is not only beautiful; it is also right and true and profound, and Jesus tells him so. "You have given the right answer," he says. "Do this, and you will live." Or did it sound more like this: "You have given the right *answer*; *do* this, and you will live"? Klunk. You have gotten the right answer; you have understood; you have said it very, very well. You know what to do, now do it. Klunk.

Why klunk? Because the lawyer thinks about all the people he passes to and from his way to work, all the people sitting on steps and sleeping on sidewalks and drinking in doorways. He thinks about the morning's headlines and about the handful of bulk letters that will be waiting for him at the office, letters asking him to send money for abused children, prisoners of conscience, Central American refugees, handicapped veterans, and the victims of a dozen deadly diseases. He thinks about all the people on his books who cannot pay him what they owe him, and the crowds more in need of free legal advice—all of this on top of his heavy responsibilities at work and at home. The lawyer thinks about all of that and his heart goes klunk because there is no way in the world he can do it all. Do this and you will live? Do this and you will *die*, of physical, emotional, and economic exhaustion.

So the lawyer does what any good lawyer should do. Desiring to justify himself, Luke says, he asks Jesus to define his terms. "And who is my neighbor?" he asks, hoping for a little help, hoping Jesus might limit his liability enough so that he has even a prayer of being able to meet it. "Who is my neighbor?" he asks, but what he really means is, "Who is *not* my neighbor? Whom may I legitimately set outside my concern and still feel good about myself?" He wants to discuss the issue, explore it with Jesus, expose the problems inherent in it until—with a little luck—it all becomes so

117

complicated that he can go home and pay his bills with a clear conscience.

Have you ever done that? Have you ever stalled for time by making simple things so complicated that you can finally throw up your hands and blame your failure to act on the lousy directions? I have. I have friends with whom I regularly complicate things. We go to lunch and stack up all the evidence we can find that homelessness is really an insoluble problem, having as much to do with addiction, mental illness, illiteracy, and the welfare system as it does with low-cost housing, so how in the world can we, two lone individuals, even begin to do anything about it? Or we compare our experience and agree that really, if we are honest, there are as many no-account poor people as there are no-account rich people, so if there is no real correlation between goodness and money, why not have money? Giving it away may make you feel better for a while, but the chances that it will really change someone else's life are slim—again, the real problems are social and political—so why not spend it on yourself, where you *know* it will be put to good use?

Now if you are having a hard time following these arguments, please understand that is the point. These are arguments designed not to make things clearer, but to make them so muddled that it becomes difficult to move, to act, to do. They are designed to make you feel as if you really understand an issue and that your heart is in the right place, which you can prove by talking about it quite intelligently, and that understanding it is really all that is required of you.

Just this week my husband Ed and I practiced this technique at home. He had read the special section in the newspaper on the environment and we were discussing the fine points of ozone depletion and the greenhouse effect. We are both genuinely concerned about what is happening; he works with manufacturers of CFC-producing equipment and I keep up my end of things by having regular nightmares about our violence toward this gorgeous world. We talked until we understood the issues, but then it got down to what we were going to do about them. Would we start using public transportation? Boycott Styrofoam packaging in any shape or form, even if it meant going from store to store looking for eggs in cardboard containers? Cut down on our own energy consumption by replacing the furnace and doing without air conditioning? Our conversation lost momentum there. Ed remembered some things he had to do in the basement and I had to get back to my sermon. Everything gets so complicated, you see, once you begin to define your terms.

But Jesus simply will not cooperate. The lawyer wants to talk about love and about how complicated it is to be open to everyone all the time, how impossible, really, and can't Jesus make the directions a little easier to follow, like defining who *is* my neighbor, exactly? But Jesus knows that the last thing on earth the lawyer needs is another discussion and a little more understanding, so he tells him a story instead, the story you already know about how it does not matter what we think, understand, know, feel, or say about love, but what we *do* about love that brings us life.

After he has told the story, he lets the lawyer answer his own question. "Which of these three," Jesus says—the two religious types who crossed to the other side of the road or the heretical outcast who took care of the beaten man— "which of these three, do you think, proved neighbor to the man who fell into the hands of the robbers?" It is a setup, of course. There is only one simple answer to Jesus' question and the lawyer, again, gives the right one: "The one who showed him mercy." The one who *did* something. "Go and *do* likewise," Jesus says back to him. "*Do* this, and you will live."

You may have noticed that it is not really an answer to the question the lawyer asks. The question he asks is, "Who is my neighbor?" But the question Jesus answers is, "Whose neighbor are you?" The answer is: anyone's. Everyone's. Jesus declines to limit the commandment of love and lets the lawyer decide how he will act upon it, but one thing is for sure. What Jesus is calling him to is not a leap of thought, or understanding, or knowledge, or emotion, but a leap of action—of showing mercy, of being a neighbor, of *doing* love.

Please don't get me wrong. This is not a sermon about doing more, or about feeling guilty if you do not. The very next story Luke tells in his gospel is about busy, busy Martha and her lazy sister Mary, whom Jesus praises for lolling at his feet while Martha does more. This is not a sermon about doing more. It is instead a sermon about not confusing the knowing, understanding, feeling, thinking, or saying of love with the *doing* of love. Those are all perfectly fine activities, but only one of them leads to eternal life, according to this story. Only one leads to the fullness of life that makes you believe there is no end to life, or to love, either, and thank God you have enough of both to go around.

So love God. Love a neighbor. *Be* a neighbor, and let us not complicate things by arguing about the specifics. You know what it means to do love because some time or another you have been on the receiving end of it, but remember that knowing the right answers does not change a thing. If you want the world to look different next time you go outside, do some love. Do a little or do a lot, but do some, and do not forget to get some for yourself. Let the summer showers of God's love soak the seeds of your right answers so that they blossom into right actions and watch the landscape begin to change. *Just do it*, and find out that when you do, you do live, and live abundantly, just like the man said.

The Opposite of Rich

When he heard this, he was shocked and went away grieving, for he had many possessions. Then Jesus looked around and said to his disciples, "How hard it will be for those who have wealth to enter the kingdom of God!"
Mark 10:22-23

Most of us know this story as the story of the rich young ruler, although Mark is the only one who suggests he is rich, Matthew is the only one who says he is young, and Luke is the only one who calls him a ruler. The fact that he shows up in all three of these gospels is a pretty good indication that his story is true, although most of us wish that he had never shown up at all. Because of him, we have one of the hardest sayings in the whole Bible, one that strikes fear in the hearts of would-be Christians everywhere: "Go, sell what you own, and give the money to the poor, and you will have treasure in heaven; then come, follow me."

Mark does not say right off that the man is rich, but you can tell. Not because he has good manners, running up and kneeling at Jesus' feet, or because he addresses Jesus so grandly once he is there—"Good Teacher"—but because of the question he asks. "What must I do to inherit eternal life?" It is a rich man's question, posed by someone whose bills are paid, whose income is secure, someone who is not preoccupied by lesser questions such as, "Where can I find a job?" or "How can I feed my family?" This man is free of those particular concerns. He does not have to spend his days trying to make ends meet in this life; he is free to pursue the good-life-to-come, secure in the knowledge that he is one of God's chosen people.

Because that is one of the things that wealth meant in his day. Not if it was gotten unfairly, of course. If wealth was gotten by lies and meanness, then it was no better than poison for those who had it. But if it was gotten fairly, by honest means, then it was seen as a sign of God's blessing. Bestowing wealth on people was one of the ways God freed them from the daily grind in order to serve the Lord. So this man approaches Jesus with no shame about his great possessions. If anything, they are his credentials, the very things that give him the right to ask his question in the first place.

But Jesus is not impressed. Looking down at the man kneeling before him, he sees someone who is clearly above average and who works hard to stay that way, someone who wants to achieve as much in heaven as he has achieved on earth and who will do whatever is required of him to add eternal life to the list of things that are his. Maybe the man hopes he will be asked to buy shoes for every man, woman, and child in Palestine or, better yet, to throw dustcovers over his furniture and put his furs in storage while he accompanies Jesus on his travels. He is an extraordinary man who wants an extraordinary assignment, but Jesus will not cooperate.

"You know the commandments," he says, and reels off half of them. Do not do this, do not do that. Honor your father and mother. Any first-grader could have recited the rest. It is the most ordinary answer imaginable, the ABC of everyday life on earth. But since the man wants something he can *do*, then that is something for him to do, same as for everyone else.

"Teacher, I have kept all these since my youth," the man says—and Jesus loves him, just like that, which is proof that the man did not say it pompously or impatiently. He said it, instead, like a confession: I have kept the Law all my life, which is how I know it is not enough. I have amassed great wealth, which is how I know that is not enough either. I am a rich man, rich in things, rich in respectability, rich in obedience to the Law. That is how I know none of those things is enough to give me the life I want. What must I do to inherit *eternal* life, the kind of life that lasts?

No wonder Jesus loves him. He is ripe. He is ready for God. He has come to the end of what he can do for himself. He has come to the end of what his church and his society can do for him. All that is left for him to do is to kneel at the feet of a street preacher with eyes like stars and ask him what to do. So Jesus looks at him, really looks at him, and he loves what he sees: a true seeker, who has kept God's word and his own, who had translated his beliefs into a life of genuine obedience to God. And who knows there is more, and who knows whom to ask about it.

But Jesus does more than look at the man. He also looks into him, deeply, like a doctor making a diagnosis. He looks inside of him to see what the matter is, where the problem is, and what is the right medicine to heal it up again. Jesus looks at him with as much compassion as he ever looked at anyone who was blind or deaf or paralyzed—aching to make him whole. Then he chooses his healing words with care.

"You lack one thing," he says, and surely the man's heart spun in place for joy. At last! Someone who sees past what he has to what he lacks and who will help him find what he is missing. Whatever it is, he will do it. Whatever it costs, he will pay it. Whatever it requires of him, he will earn it. He will do anything to add the prize of eternal life to his treasury, only it turns out not to be a matter of addition but subtraction.

"Go, sell what you own, and give the money to the poor, and you will have treasure in heaven," Jesus says to him tenderly, "then come, follow me." It is a rich prescription for a rich man, designed to melt the lump in his throat and the knot in his stomach by dissolving the burden on his back, the hump that keeps banging into the lintel on the doorway to God. It is an invitation to become smaller and more agile by closing his accounts on earth and opening one in heaven so that his treasure is drawing interest inside that tiny gate instead of keeping him outside of it. It is a dare to him to become a new creature, defined in a new way, to trade in all the words that have described him up to now—wealthy, committed, cultured, responsible, educated, powerful, obedient—to trade them all in on one radically different word, which is *free*.

It seems to me that Christians mangle this story in at least two ways. First, by acting as if it were not about money, and second, by acting as if it were only about money. It *is* about money. As far as Jesus is concerned, money is like nuclear power. It may be able to do a lot of good in the world, but only within strongly built and carefully regulated corridors. Most of us do not know how to handle it. We get contaminated by its power, and we contaminate others by wielding it carelessly ourselves—by wanting it too desperately or using it too manipulatively or believing in it too fiercely or defending it too cruelly. Every now and then someone manages to use it well, but the odds of that are about as good as they are of pressing a camel through a microchip. The story of the rich young ruler *is* a story about money.

But it is not a story that is only about money, because if it were then we could all buy our ways into heaven by cashing in our chips right now and you know that is not so. None of us earns eternal life, no matter what we do. We can keep the commandments until we are blue in the face; we can sign our paychecks over to Mother Teresa and rattle tin cups for our supper without earning a place at God's banquet table. The kingdom of God is not for sale. The poor cannot buy it with their poverty any more than the rich can buy it with their riches. The kingdom of God is God's consummate gift, to be given to whomever God pleases, for whatever reasons please God.

The catch is, you have got to be free to receive the gift. You cannot be otherwise engaged. You cannot be tied up right now, or too tied down to respond. You cannot accept God's gift if you have no spare hands to take it with. You cannot make room for it if all your rooms are already full. You cannot follow if you are not free to go.

That is why the rich young ruler went away sorrowful, if you ask me; he understood all at once that he was not free. His wealth was supposed to make him free, but kneeling in front of Jesus he understood that it was not so. Invited to follow, he went away sorrowful instead, for he had great possessions that he lugged behind him like a ball and chain. He is the only person in the whole gospel of Mark who walks away from an invitation to follow; he is the only wounded one who declines to be healed. Poverty scared him more than bondage. He could not believe that the opposite of rich might not be poor, but free.

"Then Jesus looked around and said to his disciples, 'How hard it will be for those who have wealth to enter the kingdom of God!'" They were amazed at his words, positively astonished by them, Mark says. He was challenging the social order, turning it upside down. Those who rode through the gates of Jerusalem on golden litters would find their handlebars stuck on the gates of God's kingdom. But so would everyone else who could not leave things behind.

I do not know why the disciples were so amazed, frankly. Two of them had left their fishing nets behind, two more of them a fishing boat (not to mention their father). Another one left a lucrative career, pushing his chair away from his tax collector's desk to follow the strange man with the burning eyes. All of them had walked away from something, but not because it was a prerequisite for becoming a disciple. It was more like a consequence, really. He called, they followed, and stuff got left behind. Not because it was bad, but because it was in the way. Not because they had to, but because they wanted to. He called, and nothing else seemed all that important anymore. Jesus was so much more real to them than anything else in their lives that it was no big heroic thing to follow him. He set them free, that is all. It was not their achievement. It was his gift.

I know, I know. The children, the mortgage, the aging parents, the doctor's bills, the economy, the future. I know. It's the same for me. There are days when threading a camel seems easier than following Jesus. So who *can* be saved? And who is brave enough to be free? The question has not changed much, but neither has the answer: for us it is impossible, but not for God. For God, all things are possible.

The One to Watch

He sat down opposite the treasury, and watched the crowd putting money into the treasury. Many rich people put in large sums. A poor widow came and put in two small copper coins, which are worth a penny. Mark 12:41-42

❧

What would stewardship season be without the widow's mite? It would be like Thanksgiving without turkey, Christmas without presents, Easter without eggs. The story of the widow's mite is the all-time great story of Christian giving, the story of a poor woman who gave everything she had to the church. What the rich young ruler could not do, she did without even being asked, only there was no crowd to witness the liquidation of her estate. It was as easy as uncurling her fingers from around two copper coins and letting them fall into the temple treasury, still damp from her hands, where they made such a small sound that only she could hear it.

As far as she knew, no one even saw her. But then again, no one ever saw her. She was one of life's minor characters, one of the invisible people who come and go without anyone noticing what they do, or what they have on, or when they leave the room. She was a bit player, one of the extras who ring the stage while the major characters stride around in the middle, dazzling everyone with their costumes and high drama.

In the temple scene Mark describes for us, those characters include rich people and scribes—among many, many others, but those are the ones who stand out—people who know that other people are watching them and who seem used to it, even pleased, when heads turn and talk stops for a moment as they make their entrances. Their clothes are splendid, and they fit. They do not hang on them like the clothes of the minor characters. They have shape; they have flair. When these clothes come into a room, they announce that Someone has arrived, someone whom the no-ones both envy and admire—the rich because they have money, and the scribes because they have status.

The scribes of Jesus' day were Jerusalem's elite, doctors of the law whose long years of study made them the official interpreters of God's word. They were the religious professionals, the ones to whom people turned for guidance and counsel. They were the clergy, who wore long robes, and whose names were listed in the bulletin, and whom people wanted their children to know. However, they were not paid as our clergy are. They were, in fact, forbidden to receive pay for doing their jobs, so they lived on subsidies instead— a little from their students, a little from the poor box, a little from the temple treasury.

Some scribes were not content with a little, however, and found ways to make a lot more—by using their positions to wrangle invitations to people's homes, for instance, where they accepted the best seats, the best cuts of meat, the best cups of the best wine. When they wore out their welcomes, no one dared to tell them so, least of all their poorer parishioners, who were glad to spend their savings on such esteemed guests.

So while the scribes may have been without money, they were not without honor, honor that some of them—not all of them, but some of them—turned to their own advantage. When they felt that advantage begin to slip, they could always say, "Let us pray," reminding everyone whose side they were on. Or they could spend a little more time in the temple, planting themselves there in their long, impressive robes to be seen by those who came to make their offerings to God. The scribes were clearly the people to watch. They were the guardians of the faith, the religious aristocracy, even if they did sponge off those they were meant to serve.

They were the ones to watch, only Jesus was not watching them in the temple that day. He was not paying attention to what was happening on center stage at all because he was far more interested in what was going on in the wings, and in one woman in particular. It is hard to know how she caught his attention. She did not catch anyone else's, that is for sure. She was all used up. Even a scribe could see there was no meat left in her larder; there was none left on her bones. She was out—out of food, out of money, out of what it took for a single woman to scratch her living among people who looked right through her as if she were not there. When she lost her husband, she not only lost her place and her name; she also lost her face. She had become invisible. No one saw her anymore. No one, that is, except Jesus.

He saw her walk to the temple treasury to give up her two coins, and something about the way she did it—the length of time she stood there, maybe, or the way she cradled them in her hand like her last two eggs—something about the way she did it let him know that it was the end for her, that it was everything she had, so that when she surrendered them and turned to go, he knew she had nothing left that was not God's. Her sacrifice was complete, so complete that he called his disciples over to witness it. "Truly I tell you," he said to them, "this poor widow has put in more than all those who are contributing to the treasury. For all of them have contributed out of their abundance; but she out of her poverty has put in everything she had, all she had to live on."

That is why we know about her today, that nameless woman—because she gave all the little she had, holding nothing back, which made her last penny a fortune in God's eyes. If you think tithing is heroic, try following her act. She was a percentage giver, all right—one hundred percent—but while she is generally admired for her generosity, I cannot help but wonder about that.

Are we really supposed to admire a poor woman who gave her last cent to a morally bankrupt religious institution? Was it right for her to surrender her living to those who lived better than she? What if she were someone you knew, someone of limited means who decided to send her last dollar to the 700 Club? Would that be admirable, or scandalous? Would it be a good deed or a crying shame?

Nowhere in this passage does Jesus praise the widow for what she is doing. He simply calls his disciples over to notice her, and to compare what she does with what everyone else is doing. He invites them to sit down beside him and contemplate the disparity between abundance and poverty, between large sums and two copper coins, between apparent sacrifice and the real thing. He does not put anyone in the wrong. He does not dismiss the gifts of the rich. He simply points out that the major characters are minor givers, while the minor character—the poor widow—turns out to be the major donor of them all.

It is the last of his dizzy lessons in the upside-down kingdom of God, where the last shall be first, and the great shall be the servants of all, and the most unlikely people will turn out to have been Christ himself in disguise. The poor widow is his last case in point. When he leaves the temple with his disciples that day, his public ministry is over. In four days he will be dead, having uncurled his fingers from around his own offering, to give up the two copper coins of his life.

If you ask me, that is why he noticed the poor widow in the first place. She reminded him of someone. It was the end for her; it was the end for him, too. She gave her living to a corrupt church; he was about to give his life for a corrupt world. She withheld nothing from God; neither did he. It took one to know one. When he looked at her it was like looking in a mirror at a reflection so clear that he called his disciples over to see. "Look," he said to those who meant to follow him. "That is what I have been talking about. Look at her."

He could not have picked a less likely role model for them. If he had taken a Polaroid snapshot of the temple that day and handed it to the disciples with one question written underneath—"Where is Christ in this picture?"—they would never have guessed the answer. There were *major characters* in that room, after all—doctors of the law and patrons of the arts, rich people and smart people, people with names and faces—any one of them a better bet than the thin woman in the widow's weeds, a minor character if there ever was one. "She's the one," Jesus tells them when their time is up. "The one without a penny to her name, she's the one to watch."

I wish he had said it to her. It was a great moment, in which the tragedy of her life took on the possibility of meaning. It was a great tribute to her, in which the enormity of her gift was acknowledged, only she never knew it. She walked into the temple with her last two coins in her hand and she walked out again without them, totally unaware that she was being watched. As far as she knew, no one even saw her. As far as she knew, no one ever saw her. She came in with no name and she went out with no name, but where did she go? And what did she do, once she had given her life away?

I keep thinking I see her as I drive around town. It would sound better if I told you that I have been looking for her, but that is not really true. She is not one of the people I look for; she is more like one of the people I try not to see, but now that Jesus has pointed her out to me she is harder and harder to miss. The problem is, I am never positive it is she. Only she knows that for sure, but there are certain clues I am willing to share with you.

She is not a main character, for one thing. While her appearances are memorable, they are all cameos; if you have no peripheral vision, you may miss her altogether. Sometimes she is a he, sometimes she is a child, sometimes she is even a scribe. Now you see her, now you don't. So if you want to spot her you have to watch, really watch, because you never know where she will turn up next.

The second clue is that she is usually giving something away: her time, her heart, her living, her life. The general rule is that you cannot see how much it costs her, but it is almost always more than you think.

The third clue is that what she is doing rarely makes sense by any ordinary human standard. It is as if she gets her orders from some other planet, where superior beings know things we do not yet know—such as how to let go of the little that you have in order to receive the more you do not, or how to trust what you cannot see more than you trust what you can.

That is as far as I have gotten with clues, but you can probably come up with some more of your own. Here is what you do. You sit down somewhere where you can get a good look at whatever is going on, and you pay special attention to what is happening out on the edges of your vision, where people are sometimes hard to see. Then you crunch your eyes just slightly and you ask yourself: "Where is Christ in this picture?"

Knowing Glances

"Lord, when was it that we saw you hungry and gave you food, or thirsty and gave you something to drink? And when was it that we saw you a stranger and welcomed you, or naked and gave you clothing?" Matthew 25:37-38

৯

A little over a week ago I was in Washington, DC, where I was able to visit the newly completed National Cathedral. Those of you who have been there know what a stupendous place it is. Perched on the highest hill in town, it is like something out of a dream, with towers so tall they seem part of the sky, adorned with all kinds of scrollwork, fancy finials, and wild-looking gargoyles. There are three doors at the entrance—two that are merely large and a central one that is huge—with creation scenes carved into the arches above them: the birth of the moon on the right side, the sun on the left, and in the middle, the first human beings, their graceful forms emerging from the swirling waters of creation one gorgeous torso at a time.

To step past them is to enter a sacred cave, filled with whispers and footsteps, and three tiers of stained glass windows as high as the eye can see. When the sun is right you can walk under them through pools of sapphire, ruby, and

emerald light that stain your skin, like walking through a
rainbow. But even after your eyes have adjusted it is not
possible to see the high altar from the nave. That is how big
a place it is. To see the high altar you have to travel past all
the monuments of the faith, past all the memorials to human
achievement and long-gone saints, past the statue of Abraham Lincoln and the space window and the pulpit carved
with the profiles of apostles.

Only after you have taken that walk do you arrive at the
high altar, where Jesus sits on his throne at the end of time,
surrounded by the whole company of heaven as he balances
the round earth on the palm of his hand like a ripe fruit. It is
Christ the king, preparing to judge the world, preparing to
evaluate everything that has happened since all things came
to be, and that is the brilliance of the cathedral space. Even
the most casual tourist enters through the doorway of creation and winds up at the altar of the last judgment, moving
from the beginning of time to the end, to stand before the
One who will sort out everything that has happened in between.

That is where we stand every year on the last Sunday of
the Christian year, the feast of Christ the King. There are
other days on the church calendar for worshiping Christ the
baby, Christ the teacher, Christ the physician, Christ the
friend. Today we stand before the throne to worship Christ
the king, the judge, who knows everything we have ever
done. Sobering, isn't it? As the sign over the cash register at
the National Cathedral's gift shop says, "We may not have
seen you take it, but God did." God sees. God knows. And
according to this gospel lesson, what God will do with that
knowledge on the last day is to sort us into two groups—
goats to the left and sheep to the right, goats into eternal
punishment and sheep into eternal life, depending on how
we have behaved during our lifetimes.

I do not want to spend too much time belaboring the
sheep/goat distinction. Sheep were certainly more valuable
in Jesus' time, but since this story comes from Matthew's
gospel, it really does not matter what image he uses: wheat

and tares, good seed and bad, wise maidens and foolish ones. Matthew uses all of those—and he is the only gospel writer who uses any of them—because he is very keen on making his point. Namely, that relationship with God is not a matter of *having* faith but of *doing* faith, and that those who do not will be fed like so much trash into the fire that never goes out.

Matthew gives me a pain. Life is never as clear cut as he makes it out to be; I cannot sort things out the way he does. Worse yet, whenever I am supposed to preach on a passage like this one, God seems to turn the heat up. First there were all the homeless people in Washington, twice as many as in Atlanta, standing on every street corner and pushing their paper cups in my face, begging for change. I handed over my quarters until they were all gone and then I avoided the people with the cups, just walked past them as though they were not even there. Was that the right thing to do?

Then Tuesday morning a man offered to wash my car in exchange for enough money to buy some work boots. I said yes, although the price doubled before he was through. Tuesday afternoon he came back to offer me a wax job because he needed a hard hat, too. I said yes again. Wednesday he came back for Thanksgiving grocery money and I said no. Was that the right thing to do?

Wednesday night I was standing in the checkout line at Kroger's with a twenty-five pound bag of dog food when a woman greeted me from behind. "Hello, honey," she said, and I turned around to smile at someone I had never seen before in my life. "Could you give me a dollar to buy some hot dogs?" she said, and my face fell. She had one bunch of celery in her cart. "I just wanted something for my supper," she said, and I handed her the dollar bill with an exasperated sound that I regret even now. What was the right thing to do?

Matthew would have known, which is why he gives me a pain. But Matthew also gets my attention. He seems so sure about what is right and what is wrong—about who is

THE PREACHING LIFE

blessed and who is cursed—that I get anxious about doing the right thing, about getting on God's good side, so that when my turn comes I will be sent to the right and find myself not among the doomed goats but the favored sheep.

So when I hear a story like this one I review my list. First I read it over very carefully and note that I need at least one hungry person, one thirsty one, one stranger, one naked person, one sick person, and one prisoner so that I can supply—in that order—food, drink, a warm welcome, some clothes, a hospital visit, and a prison visit. Then, presumably, I will have satisfied all the requirements for ending up with the sheep instead of the goats. Now isn't that absurd?

But—as often happens when I try to make law out of gospel—there is a problem. Because to read the story carefully is to notice that both groups were totally baffled by the verdicts they received. "When was it that we saw you?" That is what they both say to the king. The sheep did not know what they had done right any more than the goats knew what they had done wrong, which seems to suggest that God's judgment will take us all by surprise, sheep and goats alike. We can study the exam file all we want, but God only knows what will be on the final.

For the characters in the story, the biggest surprise of all seems to be that Jesus knew what they were up to when they did not think he was around. Sheep and goats alike, they thought that he occupied one space at a time just as they did, and that the way they behaved in his presence was all that really counted. Meanwhile, that left them lots of free time for being with the other people in their lives, including the ones who did not count—the little ones, the least ones—the waitresses, the door-to-door magazine salesmen, the nursing home residents, the panhandlers, the inmates, the strangers at the grocery store.

The biggest surprise of all is that such people are not unknown to the king. On the contrary, they are so close to the king that he counts everything done for them as if it had been done for him, and everything not done for them as if it had not been done for him. For sheep and goats alike, the surprise is that Jesus is not *somewhere*—he is *everywhere*—and especially with the least important people who populate our days, whoever they may be. God sees, God knows, and God will judge us according to how we behaved when we thought God was not around. "We might not have seen you, but God did."

Okay, so say that is true. Say that Jesus is present in every single person whose path crosses ours, and particularly in the least ones, the lost ones, the last ones we would ever have expected. So how do we live, knowing that? How do we find the courage to get up in the morning, knowing that every pair of eyes that pleads with us that day will be his eyes, asking us for something to eat or drink or wear, asking us for recognition, for time, for attention? That is the question, but the Bible is not a book with the answers in the back. All I know is that we are asked to wrestle with that fact, to let it challenge us and unsettle us and—who knows?—maybe even to comfort us. Jesus is so present with us, and we have such unlimited opportunities to meet him and serve him, that in some way we may never understand, everything we do or don't do affects our eternal relationship with him.

One thing is for sure. You cannot win this truth like a scavenger hunt, checking off one hungry person, one thirsty one, one sick one, and one in prison. You cannot toss a quarter in a cup or throw a dollar bill at an old woman in the grocery store and call it done. "There! There's my good deed for the day, my ticket to eternity with the sheep!" You cannot *use* people that way, and besides, emptying your pockets may not be the right thing to do.

The only way to tell if they are really Jesus' eyes is to look into them, to risk that moment of recognition that may break your heart, or change your mind, or make you mad, or make you amend your life. Whatever effect it has on you, that seems to be one thing the sheep know how to do that the goats have never tried: to *look*, to *see*, to *seek* Christ in the last, the lost, the least. I am sure Matthew would not agree with me, but if you ask me, that is enough to start with. The food, the drink, the welcome, the visit—all those things will follow in their own good time. They are necessary for life; they are not optional, but by themselves they are just quarters in a cup. Charity is no substitute for kinship. We are not called to be philanthropists or social workers, but brothers and sisters. We are called into relationship, even when that relationship is unlikely, momentary, or sad. We are called to look at each other and see Christ, who promises to be there where our eyes meet, and in that glance to teach us something we need to know.

I will tell you something you already know. Sometimes when you look into those eyes all you see is your own helplessness, your own inability to know what is right. And sometimes you see your own reflection; you see everything you have and everything you are in a stark new light. Sometimes you see such gratitude that it reminds you how much you have to be thankful for, and sometimes you see such a wily will to survive that you cannot help but admire it, even when you are the target of its ambitions.

These are all things we need to know—about Jesus, about our brothers and sisters, about ourselves—but we cannot know them if we will not look. The goats are not condemned for doing bad things, remember, but for doing nothing. They bore the hungry, the thirsty, and the stranger no malice; they simply did not see any relationship between their lives and the lives of the least. There *is* a relationship. That is both the good news and the bad news today and at the last day, when we will all stand before Christ the king and find out who we are. There is a relationship, and it is up to each one of us to decide what we will do—or will not do—about it.

Right or wrong, it helps me to remember that I am not alone. Did you notice that? The sheep and the goats both speak in unison. "When was it that we saw you?" they say, reminding me that I am part of a community, and that sometimes we can do things together that I alone cannot. We are part of one flock. I count on your courage when mine fails, and I will stand in for you when yours runs low. We can talk about what to do, and why, and how we feel about it. We can hold each other up and calm each other down. We can welcome others into our fold, pressing our limits, widening our embrace.

We can do this because we are one flock, tended and fed by the Good Shepherd who is also, I suspect, the Good Goatherd. When the time comes to sort us out, those are the eyes that will meet our eyes, the eyes of the judge who sees, who knows—who knows when we have looked and when we have looked away, who knows the last, the lost, the least—not only the ones outside of us but also the ones inside of us—and who lays down his life for us all.

The Voice of the Shepherd

Jesus answered, "I have told you, and you do not believe. The works that I do in my Father's name testify to me; but you do not believe, because you do not belong to my sheep. My sheep hear my voice. I know them, and they follow me." John 10:25-27

&

One of our favorite names for Jesus is the Good Shepherd—the Lord who lays down his life for the sheep, who knows his sheep by name and who leads them beside the still waters. All of this makes for good sermons, except that somehow or another the preacher must deal with the congregation's likeness to sheep, which does not always sit well, since most of us think of sheep as slobbering, untidy, *dumb* animals who exist only to be shaved or slaughtered.

Imagine my delight, then, when I discovered last Tuesday that someone I know actually grew up on a sheep farm in the Midwest and that according to him sheep are not dumb at all. It is the cattle ranchers who are responsible for spreading that ugly rumor, and all because sheep do not behave like cows. According to my friend, cows are herded from the rear by hooting cowboys with cracking whips, but that will not work with sheep at all. Stand behind them making loud noises and all they will do is run around behind you, because they prefer to be led. You *push* cows, my friend said, but you *lead* sheep, and they will not go anywhere that someone else does not go first—namely, their shepherd—who goes ahead of them to show them that everything is all right.

Sheep tend to grow fond of their shepherds, my friend went on to say. It never ceased to amaze him, growing up, that he could walk right through a sleeping flock without disturbing a single one of them, while a stranger could not step foot in the fold without causing pandemonium. Sheep seem to consider their shepherds part of the family, and the relationship that grows up between the two is quite exclusive. They develop a language of their own that outsiders are not privy to. A good shepherd learns to distinguish a bleat of pain from one of pleasure, while the sheep learn that a cluck of the tongue means food, or a two-note song means that it is time to go home.

In Palestine today, it is still possible to witness a scene that Jesus almost certainly saw two thousand years ago, that of Bedouin shepherds bringing their flocks home from the various pastures they have grazed during the day. Often those flocks will end up at the same watering hole around dusk, so that they get all mixed up together—eight or nine small flocks turning into a convention of thirsty sheep. Their shepherds do not worry about the mixup, however. When it is time to go home, each one issues his or her own distinctive call—a special trill or whistle, or a particular tune on a particular reed pipe, and that shepherd's sheep withdraw from the crowd to follow their shepherd home. They know whom they belong to; they know their shepherd's voice, and it is the only one they will follow.

Jesus used this image to explain to the Jews why he would not answer the question they put to him in the tenth chapter of John's gospel. It was the feast of the Dedication, John tells us—a feast better known to us as Hanukkah, that day in late December when Jews celebrate the rededication of the temple in Jerusalem. Jesus was walking in the portico of Solomon, the oldest and most revered part of the Temple, when the devout Jews who had gathered there for the festival asked Jesus the same question they had been asking him all along. "How long will you keep us in suspense?" they asked him. "If you are the Christ, tell us plainly." They wanted a definitive answer, but Jesus would not give it to them for at least two reasons.

In the first place, he knew what "Christ" meant to some of them: a warrior king, a political messiah who all of a sudden would throw off his meek disguise and grind the Romans into the dust. To say yes, I am the Christ, would only add fuel to that fire, and he did not want to do that. But Jesus also seemed to know that the question itself was a problem, that if they had to ask it at all then they would not believe the answer. If they had not been able to read the signs he had already performed, if they had not been able to understand the sermons he had already preached, then they would not be able to believe a simple, "Yes, I am the Christ." He seemed to know that they were not asking because they wanted to believe, but because they wanted to debate, talk, argue, accuse. Jesus' breath would have been wasted, and so he declined to answer their question. They could not hear him, he told them, because they were not in relationship with him. "You do not believe," he said, "because you do not belong to my sheep."

Clearly, then, this story is not about us. We are baptized, church-going, dues-paying, creed-saying *Christians*. We are here, Sunday after Sunday, celebrating the sacraments of word and table; we are in the world the rest of the week, seeking and serving Christ in all persons. If we are not his sheep, then who is? We hear his voice, and he knows us, and we follow him, and he gives us eternal life, and we shall never perish, and no one shall snatch us out of his hand. This is the Lord's flock, and we do believe because we do belong to his sheep.

Or are there some impostors in here? Are there some of you who really do not belong here, who go through the motions but who cannot say what it is you believe? You want to hear the Lord's voice but you cannot quite make it out. You wind up at the watering hole at the end of the day and you do not know whom you belong to. There are so many flocks to choose from. Some of them look fatter, some look better bred, all of them look like they know what they are doing but you. You wonder if perhaps you are a stray sheep who has somehow gotten mixed in with them, and you wonder if you would not be better off going back to the wild.

Then comes time to go home and the shepherds begin to call their sheep. You listen to their voices and you wait for that moment of recognition, for that inner voice that will tell you whose you are and where you belong, but it does not come. As the sheep move off in their tightknit flocks, each led by its own shepherd, you stand there feeling lost and you wonder, "Which one is mine? Where do I belong? What *do* I believe?"

"You do not believe," Jesus says, "because you do not belong to my sheep." What a chilling verdict that is! Yet I wonder: on what grounds do most of us doubt our membership in Christ's flock? Who keeps us out? Is it the Lord himself, blocking our way with his shepherd's staff? Or do we do it all by ourselves, disqualifying ourselves from the flock because we do not believe, or believe enough, or believe in the right way?

Most of us have pretty firm beliefs about what it means to believe. One common belief is that believers are never at a loss for words. They can say what they believe and why, and they speak about their faith in ways that move and convince others. They are never embarrassed to be asked what they believe or shy to answer; they are always articulate, and eloquent, and wise.

Then there is the belief that believers are in constant touch with God, so that they understand what happens to them every day, or at least have enough faith to accept it gracefully. Consequently, believers are never doubtful or afraid. They live in total confidence that they are in God's hands, and when they say their prayers at night God talks back to them.

Another popular belief is that believers invariably find worship a meaningful experience. They act on what they hear from the pulpit, they mean every word of the Nicene Creed, and their hearts are strangely warmed at the communion rail. Believers never lose their places in the service and they never feel bored, or cranky, or left out. They have an unfailing sense of belonging, to God and to one another.

Have I gotten to your belief about believing yet? What is it that you hold over your own head? What golden ring is it that you place just high enough so that you can never quite reach it? Is it that you do not pray enough, or witness enough, or read enough theology? Is it that you are not knowledgeable enough, or enthusiastic enough, or sure enough about what you believe? Whatever it is, please stop it. Please stop exiling yourself from the flock because of your beliefs about what it takes to belong and see if you cannot allow yourself to belong simply because God says you do.

"You do not believe, because you do not belong to my sheep," Jesus says, but *listen* to what he says. He does not say that we are in or out of the flock depending on our ability to believe, but the exact opposite, in fact. He says that our ability to believe depends on whether we are in or out of the flock, and there is every reason to believe that we are in, my woolly friends, if only because we are sitting right here with the flock this morning.

If that is the case, then chances are that the way true believers believe is the way most of us believe: valiantly on some days and pitifully on others, with faith enough to move mountains on some occasions and not enough to get out of bed on others. Since we believe in what we cannot know for sure, our belief tends to have a certain lightness to it, an openness to ambiguity and a willingness not to be sure about everything. Our belief is less like certainty than like trust or hope. We are betting our lives on something we cannot prove, and it is hard to be very smug about that. Most of the time the best we can do is to live "as if" it were all true and when we do, it all becomes truer somehow.

Our belief tends to show up in our actions more than in our words. Sometimes even we have to look at what we do to understand what we believe. We are not, at heart, believers in an institution or an ideology but in a relationship that changes from day to day and year to year. Just because we believe does not mean that we are not afraid of what might happen to us; it just means that we believe we know who will be with us when it does. Some days we are as firm in our faith as apostles and some days we are like lost sheep, which means that we belong to the flock not because we are certain of God but because God is certain of us, and no one is able to snatch us out of God's hand.

So if sometimes you have trouble hearing the voice of your shepherd, be patient with yourself—because some days it sounds like a whistle and some days like a cluck; some days it sounds like a love song and some days like a curse. It is not a voice that always speaks in words, much less complete sentences, but it can usually be heard sometime between your getting up and your lying down each day, leading you beside the still waters, restoring your soul.

Be patient with yourself, and while you are at it, be patient with the rest of us too. You cannot follow a shepherd all by yourself, after all. You are stuck with this flock, or some flock, and everyone knows that sheep are, well, sheep. They panic easily and refuse to be pushed. They make most of their decisions based on their appetites and they tend to get into head-butting contests for no reason at all. But stick with the flock. It is where the shepherd can be found, which makes it your best bet not only for survival but also for joy.

Above all, understand that you belong here, as part of the flock. If you do not believe anything else, believe that—that whether you are here because you believe or because you want to believe, you are here because you belong to God's sheep just like the rest of us. And because we do, we hear his voice, and he knows us, and we follow him, and he gives us eternal life, and we shall never perish, and no one shall snatch us out of his hand. Believe it or not, here we are, and here we belong.

The Lost and Found Department

Which one of you, having a hundred sheep and losing one of them, does not leave the ninety-nine in the wilderness and go after the one that is lost until he finds it? When he has found it, he lays it on his shoulders and rejoices.
Luke 15:4-5

ॐ

You could call the fifteenth chapter of Luke "the gospel within the gospel." Beginning with the parables of the lost sheep and the lost coin, and ending with Luke's story about the prodigal son, it is good news all the way. Everything that was lost is found. The lost sheep is returned to the flock, the lost coin is recovered by its owner, the lost son is restored to his father, and the parties go on all night long. God's talent for finding us proves greater than our talent for getting lost, and there is joy in heaven as well as on earth.

We love these stories because we imagine ourselves on the receiving end of them. I listen to the parable of the lost sheep and it is about *me*. I am the poor, tuckered-out lamb, draped across my dear redeemer's shoulders so full of gratitude and relief that I vow never to wander away from him again. Or I am the silver coin, lying in some dark corner of the universe until the good woman who will not give up on me sweeps me into the light. They are stories about me, and I treasure them, but in their original context they sounded like anything but good news to their hearers.

At the beginning of the fifteenth chapter, Jesus is criticized for the third time by the Pharisees for spending his days with sinners—lepers, tax collectors, women of the night—and not only for talking with them, but for eating with them as well, in open defiance of Jewish dietary laws. Not content with dining in their unclean homes, he has gone beyond the pale by "receiving" them—returning their hospitality and receiving them as any host would receive a guest. The sinners, needless to say, are fascinated by his treatment of them. Whatever this man has to say, they want to hear more. They draw near to him, while the scribes and Pharisees choke on their rage.

From a modern perspective, it is hard to see what the fuss is all about. Jesus the good shepherd is just doing his job. Jesus the good housekeeper is just making sure every corner has been swept, and my democratic heart goes out to all the unfortunate souls whose lives he touches. Then again, I tend to imagine good old-fashioned sinners. What is so awful about a tax collector, after all? Or a hooker with a heart of gold? Nothing, if this is a nostalgic story about the past. But if it is to bear the weight of the present and the future, then it deserves better treatment.

It deserves real characters, for one thing, real Pharisees and real sinners brought face to face with a real Jesus. I do not know how they look to you, but I imagine Jesus down at the plasma bank on Boulevard, standing in line with the hungover men waiting to sell their blood, or maybe down at the city jail shooting the breeze with the bail bondsmen who cruise the place like vultures. I imagine him at the Majestic Diner on Ponce de Leon with a crack dealer, a car thief, a prostitute with AIDS, buying them all cheese omelettes when I come in with the sixth-grade confirmation class and sit down a couple of booths away.

I imagine the kids getting a load of this and then beginning to ask me questions: "Is that who we think it is?" or "How come you warn us to stay away from people like that and there he is?" Then I imagine myself saying something to them about how those who are well do not need a physician or about how the good shepherd cares more for the one than for the ninety-nine, but the words get stuck in my throat. I could tell them this morning's parables, I suppose, but I am afraid they might get the message: that to be lost is to be precious in the sight of God, and that their good behavior rates less joy in heaven that the alleged repentance going on at that nearby table. How do you tell kids something like that? It is like telling them to get lost.

That is how it sounds to the scribes and Pharisees, anyhow. They are God-fearing believers, devoted disciples who do not merely talk about the life of faith. They live it, giving God's law their full respect and scrupulous obedience. It is not an easy life but they are willing to live it because they mean to set an example. They mean to offer a healthy alternative to the ways of the world, showing people it is both possible and pleasing to live according to God's will.

They are not uninterested in sinners, but they believe that the best way to help them is to hold up a high standard, inviting them to achieve it and letting them know where they fall short, until finally they are challenged to become the best they can be. Some people have what it takes and some, tragically, do not, but there is nothing to be gained by mixing the two. It is the kind of message that appeals to people. It makes the rules clear and rewards those who obey them, admitting the winners to the ranks of the educated, the employed, the righteous, and sending the losers back to try, try again. They each stick with their own kind and they know who they are. The righteous know that they give heaven reason to rejoice and the sinners know that they grieve the heart of God, if God knows or cares who they are at all.

Then Jesus comes along and starts messing around with the system, treating sinners like special cases and making

them think they are as important as other people. He social-
izes with them, which is as good as condoning their behavior, and thereby robs them of their motivation to do better.
Why should they buy anything from the Pharisees that Jesus
is giving away for free? All they have to do is wander off
from the flock, pursuing their own whims, and the good
shepherd will go off after them, leaving the ninety-nine to
fend for themselves. It is not only bad shepherding; it is bad
pastoral care. It is bad theology. If you receive sinners and
admonish the righteous—when the system is clearly set up
to work the other way around—then what will happen to
the community of faith? What about the good people? What
about us?

These two parables are full of problems, not least of
which is that they do not seem to mean what Jesus says they
mean. According to his explanations, they are about
heaven's joy over one repentant sinner, but the lost sheep
does not repent as far as I can tell and the lost coin certainly
doesn't. They are both simply found—not because either of
them does anything right, but because someone is deter-
mined to find them and does. They are restored thanks to
God's action, not their own, so where does repentance come
in at all?

Three possibilities occur to me. First, that Jesus was just
making it all up as he went along and got his wires a little
crossed. The stories mean what he says they mean and we
should not get hung up on the details. Second, that Jesus
told the stories exactly as we have them and was content to
let us figure them out for ourselves, but that their open-end-
edness made his editors so anxious that the explanations
were added later so that we would not, um, misunderstand
them. Third, that they are not parables about lost sheep and
lost coins at all, but parables about good shepherds and dili-
gent sweepers.

"Which one of you," Jesus says, "having a hundred
sheep...." He is not inviting the Pharisees to imagine themselves sheep but to imagine themselves shepherds, leaving
their carefully tended flock in order to chase one stray

through the wilderness. Isn't it interesting the way we listen to parables like this one and can always find some way to wind up on the sheep's end of things instead of the shepherd's?

If you are willing to go with the third possibility—if you are willing to be a shepherd—then the story begins to sound different. The accent in what Jesus says falls on a different syllable. Repentance is not the issue, but rejoicing; the plot is not about amending our evil ways but about seeking, sweeping, finding, rejoicing. The invitation is not about being rescued by Jesus over and over again, but about joining him in rounding up God's herd and recovering God's treasure. It is about questioning the idea that there are certain conditions the lost must meet before they are eligible to be found, or that there are certain qualities they must exhibit before we will seek them out. It is about trading in our high standards on a strong flashlight and swapping our "good examples" for a good broom. It is about discovering the joy of finding.

A few summers ago, my husband Ed and I went on a ten-day hike in the wilderness with fifteen other people and a trip leader, none of whom we knew ahead of time. We were a motley crew from all over the United States, and as the days passed it became apparent that all walkers are not created equal. Some of us charged ahead while others of us lagged behind, and while we encouraged one another along, we soon learned that we could only travel as fast as our slowest member.

Her name was Pat. She was the eldest member of the group, and the heaviest, and the most unpleasant. She liked to walk alone at the rear of the group, which was just as well, since she had an irritating habit of listening in on other people's conversations and then breaking in to correct their grammar, geography, history, botany, or any of the other subjects about which she knew so much. She liked a full hour for lunch and threatened to be sick if she were rushed. Most of the spots our trip leader picked to stop were too sunny, or too wet, or too steep for her, but she would plunk herself down anyway and announce that she would "make do."

Around the fifth day out we got good and lost, walking for close to ten hours over three mountains before we made camp. When we arrived—after dark, in the rain, in the middle of nowhere—Pat was not with us. We compared notes and discovered that no one had seen her since noon, when she had thrown rocks at the person assigned to bring up the rear of the group and told him to leave her alone.

Delighted, he had complied, but that meant no one had seen her for almost eight hours. We were all trembling with exhaustion and soaked to the bone; no one could even imagine heading back up the last mountain in order to find her. But it was the trip leader's job, so he did it. Armed with hot soup, a jacket, and a first-aid kit, he disappeared into the dark while the rest of us milled around, trying to stay away from the idea of what it would be like to be lost in the wilderness without a match or a map or a friend.

We paced and dozed until close to midnight, when Pat stumbled into camp hanging on to her shepherd. Those of us who had despised her at noon fell all over her in the dark, petting her and hugging her and welcoming her home, pressing mugs of hot chocolate into her hands and oatmeal cookies into her pockets. No one thought to ask her if she was going to be a nicer person from now on, or whether she had learned her lesson. We were too glad to have her back. Imagining her out there in the dark, we had all felt more than a little lost ourselves, so finding her was as good as being found.

Pat acted rather nonchalant about the whole thing, if you ask me, but the next morning she was up and dressed and on the trail before any of us, and from that day on she was part of the flock. Not everybody's favorite member, by any means, but part of the flock. Maybe it was getting lost that changed her—although she denied even a moment's fear during her ordeal—but then again, maybe it was being found that did the trick. Maybe it was our welcome home that made the difference, that convinced her she was part of the flock, but at any rate it was hard to separate her repentance from ours, or the repentance from the rejoicing. We all kept better track of each other from then on, and took turns walking with Pat, who surprised everyone by bursting into song one night and leading us all in a medley of old camp tunes.

Maybe some of us are destined to be shepherds and others of us to be lost sheep, but when I am working so hard to find and stay found, it is difficult not to judge those who seem to capitalize on staying lost. I want to believe that they are not merely lost people, but that they are bad people, because then I could write them off and save myself some grief. I want to concentrate on the good people, the ones who want to be found, or who are busy finding others. I think about heaven ignoring those good folks in favor of one sinner who finally says, "I'm sorry," and I want to sue God for mercy.

Then I hear someone behind me who calls me by my name, and big brown hands grab me by the scruff of the neck, hauling me through the air and laying me across a pair of shoulders that smell of sweet grass and sunshine and home, and I am so surprised, and so relieved to be *found* that my heart feels like it is being broken into, broken open, while way off somewhere I hear the riotous sound of the angels rejoicing.

None of Us is Home Yet

Look at the birds of the air; they neither sow nor reap nor gather into barns, and yet your heavenly Father feeds them. Are you not of more value than they? Matthew 6:26

છે

Not too long ago, I took part in the blessing of a friend's home. It was not her home, really. It was a small yellow brick bungalow with a "For Sale" sign in the yard, a house lent to her by the owner while she was between jobs. The real estate agent thought the house would "show" better with someone in it, and my friend was that someone. Unsure how long she would be able to stay, unsure where she would go when the house sold and she had to leave, and fundamentally unsure about her ability to make her own living, she moved her things into the house and invited her friends to supper.

Everyone brought a dish, or a fistful of flowers, or a small gift, and after we had all eaten well we gathered in the living room to begin the celebration. The prayer book we used suggested several readings for the blessing of a home, and out of these we chose two. First we read the story from Genesis about Abraham's hospitality to the three strangers who stopped by his tent under the oaks of Mamre, and after that came a reading from the sixth chapter of Matthew's gospel.

It was somewhat shocking, under the circumstances. We had just gotten our friend settled. We had just put the books onto the shelves and hung the curtains on the windows and lined up the cans in the cupboards. We had just achieved the semblance of a home for her, even though we all knew it was no lasting home, and it would have been nice to hear a gospel lesson that said, in effect, "You are safe now. You have a place to live and everything will be all right now." That is not what it said.

You know what it said. "Therefore I tell you, do not worry about your life, what you will eat or what you will drink, or about your body, what you will wear. Is not life more than food, and the body more than clothing?" The words fell like stones in deep water. No one coughed or cleared a throat as Jesus preached to us, assuming that we believed him, assuming that we took God's providence for granted. He was telling our friend that she *was* safe, but not because she had a roof over her head and a key to the front door. "You are safe," Jesus told her, "because the God who made you will not abandon you. That is your home, which nothing and no one can take away from you."

"Oh," my friend said at the end of the reading. "Oh."

It was a more faithful response than my own. When I hear that passage I generally want to argue, not only for myself but for the whole worried world. "Yes, but...." That is what I want to say. "Yes, that is a lovely passage and I really do believe it on some level, but birds do not have bills to pay and lilies do not get arrested for loitering and the grass of the field does not have three children under five to feed and diaper. Yes, God will provide, but meanwhile there are people sleeping between cardboard sheets and eating out of garbage cans who seem to have fallen between the cracks of this passage."

Do not worry? I *do* worry. About the growing number of people in this country who have nowhere to call home, about the revolution that must take place before that trend will reverse itself, and about how I can know all of that and still enjoy my own home, which is so important to me. My house is much more than my residence. It is my sanctuary, the place where I rest, where I retire beyond the reach of the noisy world, where I am fed. It is where my bed is, and my books and my Great-Aunt Alma's quilts; it is where I bathe and sleep and dream and rise. It is where I invite my friends and where I cook for them. It is where I plant red tulips and where purple finches crowd the feeders outside my windows. It is the place my husband and I have made with and for each other over the past ten years. It is our home.

My home is a promise I make to myself when I get too tired to go on. "You can go home soon," I tell myself, and the knowledge spreads through me like sun on a cold day so that I *can* go on, for a little longer at least. Several months ago I acted on that promise, leaving the church a little before dark after a long, hard day. Looking out into the parking lot I saw my lone car. I also saw Luther, a homeless man who spends his days walking between the big downtown Atlanta churches in shoes that do not fit. He drinks, and he has lung cancer, and he loves churches.

"Hello, Luther," I said. He was sitting in the bushes with a bottle in a paper bag. "Hello, Barbara," he said. I asked him how he was and got the full answer. None of it made much sense, but then the bottle was empty and things never seemed to get any better for Luther. Finally I wearied of his monologue and said, "Luther, I've got to go home now." No sooner had I said it than I regretted it. What a thing to say to someone who did not have one! What an excuse to use with him. The word hung between us for a moment until Luther brushed it aside. "This is my home," he said, waving his arm toward the church. "This is the only home I have."

Home. What a compelling, elusive word that is. What a strong hunger the human heart has for home, and what a hard thing it is to find and keep a home—not just a building, but a place to belong—a place to *be from* and a place to *go to*. A safe place where one is known and a safe place from which to know the world: a nest, a family, a stable fortress in a vast and often frightening universe.

I had lots of homes, growing up. My family moved eleven times during my first fourteen years; I lived in six different states and went to eight different schools. I left the state where I was born when I was six months old and have never been back. When people ask me where I am from, I hesitate. Shall I lie, or bore them to tears with the truth? "I am not from anywhere, really." That is what I usually say. "We moved a lot."

And I was not alone. We live in a transient society, full of corporate nomads with children who are good at memorizing new addresses and telephone numbers, children who grow up with plenty of houses but no clear sense of home. But it is not necessary to move a lot to lose track of home these days. You can stay put right where you are and still feel the ground shift under your feet.

The neighborhood where you have lived all your life begins to change complexion; property values go way up or way down. Where did home go? The marriage breaks up and the children become commuters, living part-time with each parent. Where did home go? Or your own parents die, and the house you grew up in is taken apart piece by piece. Where did home go?

None of our sanctuaries is invincible. Even the church—the one place that *should* be safe—is subject to the diverse and fractured world in which we live. Brought together by our wish to belong to one family, we sit down around the dinner table and find that we do not agree about what to believe, or how to worship or even about who belongs to the family. We confess that there is one head of our household, but our descriptions of who that is bear little resemblance to one another. Where did home go?

For as long as God's people can remember, they have been seeking the way home. "A wandering Aramean was my father...." That is how the story of Israel begins in the book of Deuteronomy, and that is the story every Hebrew learned to repeat when presenting first fruits to the Lord. However settled God's people became, however prosperous they became in their promised land, they were not to forget the long roundabout journey by which they had been delivered there. Wanderers once, they would be wanderers again, but wherever they went they were to remember: their destination was never Egypt or Jerusalem or Babylon but God, always God.

Thousands of years later, Jesus would appear, a messiah with a house but no home. "Foxes have holes, and birds of the air have nests; but the Son of man has nowhere to lay his head," he says in the ninth chapter of Luke (9:58). It is not a complaint; it is the truth. If God is where we came from and God is where we are going, then we have no permanent address and all our shelters along the way are temporary ones. Our houses, our church buildings, our offices—even this lovely old chapel—they are all good places to park ourselves and rest a while, but they are not good places to define ourselves by, or sustain ourselves with, because they do not have that kind of power.

On any given night, however comfortable we may be and however secure our futures may seem, we remain vulnerable to a certain heaviness of heart that can come upon us for no apparent reason at all. It may begin as a flutter in the chest or as a full-blown ache—a sudden hollowness inside, a peculiar melancholy, an inexplicable homesickness. Have you felt it? The sense that there is a place you belong that you have somehow gotten separated from, a place that misses you as much as you miss it and that is calling you to return, only you do not know where, or how to get there. All you know is that you are not there yet, and that your life will not be complete until you are.

It is not the best feeling in the world, but it is not the worst either. It is not a bad thing to know you belong somewhere, even if you are not there yet. I like to think of it as God's tug, a kind of homing instinct planted in each one of us that nags at us, and turns us around, and makes us restless when we sit still too long, because none of us is home yet. That is the deep truth. Some of us have houses and some of us do not; all of us stake out various places to be for days, or months, or years, but none of us is home yet.

A wandering Aramean was our father; our Lord had nowhere to lay his head. We have loved him without having seen him, as Saint Peter wrote almost two thousand years ago, and it is truer now than it was then. We have loved him without having seen him, but we mean to see him. We track him, following his fresh prints out of our churches and into the streets, into the projects, into the courts. We track him to all the places where people stand in long lines with pieces of dirty paper folded in their hands, all the places they bend over lengthy application forms with ballpoint pens that do not work.

We track him in their faces, which are surprising in their variety. We look for him in the veteran, the widow, the immigrant, the young mother with the crowd of children around her legs. We seek him in the big-shouldered man in the wheelchair, the grandmother with the large flowered bag over her arm, the Native American whose sleek black braid reaches halfway down his back. We follow him by following them home, or following them into all the places they live that are not home for them. When we join them there, it dawns on us that the body of Christ is fundamentally homeless—as strange as it sounds, the only reason he can make his home everywhere is that he calls no place home—and that we who belong to his body are as footloose as our Lord.

What that means for the church is that homelessness is not an "issue" for us that we attend to merely out of social conscience; it is our primary identity, and when we forget that we forget who we are and whom we follow. We also, I think, forget how to serve. Ignoring the truth about ourselves, we cling to certain illusions that foul us up and wear us down, turning our service of God into a panicky duel with our own devils.

We cling to the illusion that some of us are blessed and some of us are not, and that it is our job as those who are blessed to rescue those who are not. We labor under the illusion that our work involves "us" and "them," with us—the caregivers, the helpers, the lucky—on one side of the counter and them—the clients, the supplicants, the unlucky—on the other. We succumb to the illusion that they can all be saved if only we will work enough hours, find enough money, get enough publicity.

We may also cling to our own comforts, more aware than ever how much they matter to us, and we may try to cut deals with God: that if we are allowed to keep what we have then we will double our efforts on behalf of those who have less than we do. Meanwhile we can hardly enjoy what we do have for all the guilt it provokes in us. Shall we cut our own rations to bread and water? Wear sackcloth to work? What shall we do?

"Therefore I tell you, do not worry about your life, what you will eat or what you will drink, or about your body, what you will wear. Is not life more than food, and the body more than clothing?" That is what we shall do. When we forget who we are, our Lord reminds us: we are the people who live by the grace of God alone, by trusting in God's providence and by remembering that we are more, far more, than what we consume or wear or where we live. We may care for ourselves and we may care for others, but it is God who cares for us all, and none of us is home yet.

If we remember that, our service to others will be as different as our sense of ourselves. There is no "us" or "them" out there, just us—all of us—lined up on the same side of God's counter. Some have more than others, but we are all blessed, all called to bless one another, all seeking the way home and finding it in one another's company. We do not have to wear ourselves out protecting ourselves from the truth—that none of us is home yet, that home is hard to find, that our longing for home is deep and abiding and often very, very painful. We do not have to use up all our energy running from that fact, or running from those who remind us of it.

We can instead choose to serve those among us who are closest to that truth, who live out our homelessness for us in very literal, concrete ways. We can join them in their search for a home, understanding that their search is our own search. We can serve the God who feeds and clothes and shelters by doing some of that ourselves, but always with the knowledge that it is God who provides—no—who *is* our true and only home, in whose household there is plenty— for the birds of the air, for the lilies of the field, and for every one of us.

The Prodigal Father

Then Jesus said, "There was a man who had two sons.
The younger of them said to his father, 'Father, give me
the share of the property that will belong to me.' So he di-
vided his property between them." Luke 15:11-12

❧

Most of us grew up calling Jesus' story about a
man and his two sons the Parable of the Prodigal
Son, but it is not. Jesus does not begin his tale by
saying, "There once was a man who had a father and an
elder brother...."

"There was a man who had two sons," he says, letting us
know whom the story is really about—a father who loved
his two children to distraction and wanted them to love
each other too. The story is one of three that he tells in a row
after the Pharisees and scribes have taken him to task for
eating with sinners. Jesus does not argue with them. He tells
them stories instead, about a shepherd who left ninety-nine
sheep to fend for themselves while he went after one stray,
about a woman who turned her house upside down in order
to find one lost coin, and about a compassionate father who
dealt graciously with his two sons. All three stories address
the Pharisees' concern that Jesus is condoning sin by keeping the company he keeps, and all three reply that God is

too busy rejoicing over found sheep, found coins, and found children to worry about what they did while they were lost.

If you are familiar with the Episcopal Church's prayer book service for the reconciliation of a penitent, then you know that the parable of the loving father is how that service ends. After you have confessed your sins, promising to turn again to the Lord and to forgive those who have sinned against you, the priest lays a hand on your head and absolves you in the name of God, saying, "Now there is rejoicing in heaven; for you were lost, and are found; you were dead, and now are alive in Christ Jesus our Lord. Go in peace. The Lord has put away all your sins."

Those are powerful words that sum up a powerful sacrament, but according to the parable they are used out of context. According to the parable, no confession is necessary, no promise of better behavior in the future, no forgiveness of those who have sinned against you. According to the parable, you do not even have to make it into the church. The loving father who sees you coming while you are still at a distance will rush out to embrace you, and kiss you, and forgive you before you can get a word out of your mouth.

While that may be excellent news for the prodigals among us, it is also disturbing news, because forgiveness is one of those gifts of God that cuts both ways. Forgiveness is right, right? We are all in need of it, and when we get it, from God or from one another, we know what new life is all about. But forgiveness is forgiveness of sin and sin is wrong, right? In order to be forgiven, someone has to have fallen short of the glory of God, which may be as simple as having failed to be kind to someone, but which may also be as complicated as having killed someone. Whatever the crime, very few of us would deny the possibility of forgiveness, but most of us would insist on penance, on the sinner's heartfelt confession and willingness to pay for the wrong that has been done. Then along comes this story of instant forgiveness with no strings attached, and we cannot miss the point:

that the extravagant love of God both fulfills and violates our sense of what is right.

Preachers and teachers often insult this parable by turning it into a cartoon, in which a sulking, mean-spirited older brother begrudges the love a father shows for a reckless, fun-loving younger brother who has come home. But that is entirely too simple, and Jesus said nothing of the kind. Instead, he told a darker story, a story about a younger son who was so hungry to see the world that he wished his own father dead—at least symbolically—by asking him to settle his estate early and give both brothers their share. So the father—apparently valuing his child's freedom more than his own security—divided his livelihood and said goodbye to his younger son, who went off and squandered everything, until one day he "came to himself." That was when he decided to go back home, composing a pretty calculated confession as he went, one designed to get him back with a roof over his head and food in his belly even if it meant he had to live as a servant and not as a son.

He came home, in other words, to live off his *brother's* inheritance, having spent his own in loose living, and no sooner did his father see him coming down the road than the elder brother's fatted calf was killed and the celebration was on. There were no extra steps between the younger son's return and his welcome home party, no heart-to-heart with the old man, no extra chores, no go-to-your-room-for-a-week-and-think-about-what-you-have-done, just a clean robe for his back, and a fine ring for his hand, and a pair of new sandals for his feet. The father did not even wait for his elder son to get home from work before beginning the festivities, "for this son of mine was dead and is alive again; he was lost and is found!" Then the elder brother came home from the fields, heard the music and the dancing, and I am glad that I was not the one who had to tell him what it was all about.

I am an eldest child myself, after all. I know what it is like to break parents in, to step aside as they exercise their new and improved skills on younger siblings, and then to take the rap for the little criminals when they mess up. I remember when I was nine years old, a third-grader at Fernbank Elementary School, and my sisters Kate and Jennifer were seven and three. One Saturday afternoon when I was supposed to be looking after them, my parents came home early and within minutes had hauled me by my elbow to the upstairs bathroom, where they pushed open the door and showed me one of the most awful sights I had ever seen: my little sister Jennifer, clutching a fat black Crayola crayon in her fist, putting the finishing touches on the claw-footed porcelain bathtub that had once been white. Did she get spanked? No, she was just a little baby who did not know any better. Did I get spanked? Yes, I was the older sister who should have kept her out of trouble.

Older siblings frequently get the raw end of the deal, as the elder brother apparently does in the parable at hand. My guess is that he was not incensed by his younger brother's return, or even by his father's forgiveness of him, but by the celebration. Let the penitent come home, by all means, but let him come home to *penance*, not a party. Where is the moral instruction in that kind of welcome? What about facing the consequences of your actions? What about reaping what you sow? What kind of world would this be if we all made a practice of rewarding sinners while the God-fearing folk are still out in the fields?

I mean, what do you have to do to get a little attention around here? The church thrives on its ministries to the poor, the broken, the sick and outcast, but what about those of us who are holding our own? What about those of us who are burning our candles at both ends, trying to serve God and keep up with our other responsibilities, too? What about those of us who work hard to keep our jobs and stay in our relationships and take care of our health and pay our dues, but never seem to get any credit for it, while the homeless and the addicted and the downtrodden get all the attention? What do you have to do to get a party around here? Do you have to go off and squander your inheritance before you can come home to be embraced, and kissed, and assured that you belong?

"Listen!" the elder son protests. "For all these years I have been working like a slave for you, and I have never disobeyed your command; yet you have never given me even a young goat so that I might celebrate with my friends. But when this son of yours came back, who has devoured your property with prostitutes, you killed the fatted calf for him!" God help the elder son. God help him, and God help all of us who understand his rage, who have felt so excluded and whose hurt has run so deep that we have cut ourselves off from the very ones whose love and acceptance we so desperately need. "This son of *yours*," the elder brother says, excluding himself from the family—this son of yours who is no kin to me, nor am I kin to you if you are going to choose him over me.

But here is where the loving father earns his title. He does not take a swing at his firstborn, as some of us might have been tempted to do, nor even remind him to honor his father. He knows that he has lost both of his sons. He has lost the younger one to a life of recklessness, but he has lost the older one to a more serious fate, to a life of angry self-righteousness that takes him so far away from his father that he might as well be feeding pigs in a far country. He wants his father to love him as he deserves to be loved, because he has stayed put, and followed orders, and done the right thing.

He wants his father to love him for all of that and his father *does* love him, but not for any of that, any more than he loves the younger brother for what he has done. He does not love either of his sons according to what they *deserve*. He just loves them, more because of who he is than because of who they are, and the elder brother cannot stand it. He cannot stand a love that transcends right and wrong, a love that throws homecoming parties for prodigal sinners and expects the hard-working righteous to rejoice. He cannot stand it and so he stands outside—outside his father's house and outside his father's love—refusing his invitation to come inside.

But his father turns out to be prodigal too, at least as far as his love is concerned. He never seems to tire of giving it away. "Son," he says, reclaiming the boy, "you are always with me, and all that is mine is yours." His love for one child does not preclude his love for the other. The younger one's recklessness cannot deflect it any more than the elder one's righteousness. They are a family; they belong to one another, and a party for one is a party for all. "We had to celebrate and rejoice," the loving father says to his elder son, "because this brother of yours"—not *my* son but *your* brother—"was dead and has come to life; he was lost and has been found."

It is the elder brother's invitation back into relationship not only with the loving father, but also with the wayward brother. It is an invitation to recognize his own lostness and foundness, but the parable does not tell us how it all turned out. The story ends with the elder brother standing outside the house in the yard with his father, listening to the party going on inside. Jesus leaves it that way, I think, because it is up to each one of us to finish the story. It is up to each one of us to decide whether we will stand outside all alone being right, or give up our rights and go inside to take our place at a table full of reckless and righteous saints and scoundrels, brothers and sisters united only by our relationship to one loving father, who refuses to give us the love we deserve but cannot be prevented from giving us the love we need.

Surviving Eden

*So when the woman saw that the tree was good for food,
and that it was a delight to the eyes, and that the tree was
to be desired to make one wise, she took of its fruit and
ate; and she also gave some to her husband, who was with
her, and he ate.* Genesis 3:6

જી

Every family has its stories—how Grandmother met
Grandfather, how they courted and wed. How the
first house burned to the ground and all was lost;
how the neighbors showed up next day with timber and
nails and hope was rebuilt. How the children fought and
grew; how Uncle Billy never really did, living at home until
he died an old man, as sweet and simple as the day he was
born.

My mother is working on our family history, calling up
distant relatives and filling in missing branches on the family tree. A couple of weeks ago my telephone rang. "Bad
news," she said. "Moonshiners. Potato farmers. A chain
gang boss. All I can find out about one guy is that he took
his cow everywhere he went. People would hear a bell in
the middle of the night and look out their windows to see
Cousin Ezra walking his cow in the dark."

Recently her spirits have improved. "I think I found revo-
lutionary war heroes!" she exclaimed. "On my father's

mother's side. She married below her class, but who cares? Physicians! Artists! Teachers!" Every family has its stories: tragedies, comedies, tall tales, legends. Good or bad, they matter to us because they explain us somehow. They help us find our places in the history of the world—these are my people and this is how they lived—and in many cases they help us understand why we are the way we are. Telling family stories, we rehearse the family virtues and reveal the family flaws. We discover things about ourselves as we do, and one thing in particular: that even when we think we have the stage all to ourselves and are acting on our own, there is nothing new under the sun. We are simply the most recent players in the age-old dramas of life and death that unite us to every other human being who ever walked the earth.

This first story from the book of Genesis is one of those, an ancient family story that seems to tell us some true things about ourselves and about our ambition and appetite, our curiosity and daring, about how blindly we can make life-changing decisions and how sorry we can be once we see what we have done. Most of us learned the story when we were very young as the story of the fall, about how Adam and Eve fell from the grace of eternal life in paradise to everyday hell on earth through their disobedience. The picture in the storybook Bible filled me with awe: a naked man and woman being driven by angels with flaming swords from a beautiful garden, their pitiful hands covering their shameful heads.

Few of our teachers could resist adding a moral to the story. If we did not want to suffer a similar fate, they warned us, then we had better obey our elders, who were after all God's representatives on earth. Didn't it go something like that? Or maybe you learned a slightly more sophisticated version when you were a little older, that the story of the fall is the story of how original sin came into the world. Because Adam and Eve made the decision they did, we are somehow contaminated by our kinship with them,

169

infected with congenital germs of evil and death that are always waiting to break out in us if we are not very stern with ourselves, if we do not remain on our best and most holy behavior.

But neither of these readings is supported by the text itself. Nowhere in all the Bible, in fact, are the words "fall" or "original sin" ever used to refer to this story. Both of those are labels that were applied much, much later, in an effort to make *sense* of the story, to discover its meaning and learn its lesson so that humankind would not keep on falling forever.

But the story itself is not concerned with such things. It is not a thinly disguised piece of systematic theology. It is a story about God and about humankind, about a choice and its consequences. It is one of the family stories that tells us things about ourselves we need to know. It tells us not only how we fail—we already know that very well—but also how we survive. Because that is part of the story too, you know. Adam and Eve did not die at the end of it. They went on, but how? That is what I want to know. How did they go on after they had defied the God who was not only their maker but also their only friend? How did they fashion a future from such a short and sorry past? And how in the world did they live through the loss of paradise?

Paradise. Even for those of us who have never been there, the word conjures up green ferns, blue skies, bright water, warm breezes—peace and plenty of it, plenty of everything, including the strong, kind presence of God. Paradise was that place where there was no fear or shame, where there was nothing to hide and nothing to hide from. It was a place where nothing had ever been broken, where there were no chips or dents or scars, a place where everything was still whole and holy and pleasing to God.

The best way the writer of Genesis could think of to describe it was to say that paradise was the kind of place where you could walk around naked, where you could skinny-dip to your heart's content. It was that safe—so safe, in fact, that it might never even occur to you that you *were* naked, at least as long as you stayed away from the fruit of one particular tree.

But you know the story. Eve did not stay away. She and the serpent engaged in the first religious debate recorded in history, after which she bit into the fruit of the one particular tree and nothing was ever whole again. Paradise was lost, and there was no going back.

Do you know the feeling? As in a dream, you watch your hand reach out to cradle the bright, heavy fruit, knowing you are not even hungry, knowing it is not yours to take but taking it anyhow. Your muscles are on remote control, your mind is a buzzing hive, your heart is on hold. You take, you eat, and it is very good, but before you can swallow it things have already begun to change. The light has gone dull. The wind has stopped. Your hands are sticky, and heavy as wood. You look down at them and find that you are naked—it is one of *those* dreams—so you try to cover yourself and then to run, but it is no use. You are stuck, rooted to the spot, exposed for anyone who passes by to see.

Actually, if it had happened that way for Adam and Eve their story might have had a different ending, but when they discover that they are naked they do manage to cover themselves and then to run away and hide, so that when the Lord God seeks their company in the cool of the day he has to look for them. "Where are you?" he asks, and the alibis begin to fly. Adam blames God for giving him Eve, and then blames Eve for handing him the fruit, while Eve blames the serpent for tricking her. Nothing is sacred, apparently. These two are willing to sacrifice their integrity, their relationship, and their dominion over the garden in their frantic efforts to cover their nakedness, all of which gets them nowhere. Beginning with the serpent, the Lord God delivers their sentences: pain for Eve, toil for Adam, dust to dust for them both.

And of course God was right—is God ever wrong?—but still, what a colossal loss, what a mortal blow. You give in to one crazy, selfish desire, you look away from the light for one moment—and the car crashes, the job vanishes, the relationship ends, and there is no going back. Paradise is lost and what was, or what could have been, is gone forever. How do you *survive* something like that?

Well, there are a couple of ways, actually. You can, as we have seen, find someone else to blame for what has happened to you. That way you get to be angry instead of hurt and afraid, but you are also able to remain a victim. If someone else has ruined your life, after all, then it is up to someone else to repair it, which does not leave you much to do but sit around and wait to be fixed.

On the other hand, you can blame yourself, punishing yourself in a number of different ways. You can keep track of your failures, for instance, withdrawing from life a little more with each one of them until you are afraid to come out of hiding long enough to try anything at all. Or you can take the opposite tack, driving yourself harder and harder to make up for your losses, settling for nothing less than perfection in yourself and those around you.

You can blame paradise itself, convincing yourself that it was not so hot after all, or you can blame God, pointing out that he is the manufacturer, after all, and that if he expects us to be different then he should have made a different world in the first place. Who, for instance, made the snake?

There are legends about what happened to Adam and Eve that never made it into the Bible, whole books about them that were not respectable enough to become Holy Scripture, but stories with the ring of truth to them nonetheless. According to one of them, God gave Adam and Eve a cave to live in just east of Eden, where they sat in shock for months after their eviction from paradise, reciting every detail they could remember to each other: the shade of the trees, the warmth of the sun, the beauty of the land. Eve offered to kill herself if God would let Adam back into the garden alone, but Adam would not hear of it, although he tried to end his own life soon after by jumping off a cliff. When both of them had failed to die, they wept and beat their breasts and both together begged God to let them return to

172

Eden. But God said, with enormous divine sadness, that it was impossible—that once he had given his word even he could not take it back.

Instead he sent them angels to sing to them and sprinkle scented water on them to cool them. He reconciled the beasts of the earth to them, telling the animals to be gentle with them, but Adam and Eve could not be roused from their despair. For eighty-three days they languished, refusing all food and drink for fear they would sin again. God gave them a fountain of living water to drink, but took it back when they tried to drown themselves in it. He sent them figs from the garden to eat, big as watermelons, but they left them for the crows.

Finally, the legend goes, when their bodies were stained from exposure and they were speechless with heat and cold, Adam and Eve let God teach them how to sew, using thorns for needles and sheepskins to make shirts for themselves to cover their nakedness. It was a big step. Having lost paradise, having run out of bushes and alibis to hide behind, having all but killed themselves through guilt and exposure, Adam and Eve decided to let God clothe them. "Fear not," an angel sang to them that night, "the God who created you will strengthen you."

And so God did. Although the snake continued to plague them all their days, Adam and Eve decided to live. The days of peace and plenty were gone for good, but they got by. Using all the scraps at hand, they managed to build first an altar and then a home, to bake bread from the wild wheat of the field and to bear five children. Using the pieces of their broken past, they made a future for themselves and for their descendants in the world outside of Eden, a world we continue to live in today. It is a world full of chips and dents and scars. Even where we have glued it back together you can still see the cracks, but in its own way it is lovely, a mosaic of many colors, a mended work of art, a testament to the God who is willing to work with broken pieces and who calls us to do the same.

That is our story, a story with everything human in it—promise, failure, blame, guilt, forgiveness, healing, hope—a story about us and a story about our God, who did not create us just once but goes on creating us forever, putting our pieces back together so that we are never ruined, never entirely, and never for good.

Whenever the people of God gather around an altar to be fed, they do roughly the same thing. First they hear the biblical story—their story—and then they pray, and then someone holds up the bread—the round, whole, perfect symbol of God's presence among us. Then, at the very crescendo of the service, the person holding the bread breaks it into pieces, reminding us that our wholeness does not lie behind us but ahead of us, in the company of the Lord who made us, who feeds us and clothes us, and who dwells among us this side of Eden until he can bring us home.

Cowley Publications is a ministry of the Society of St. John the Evangelist, a religious community for men in the Episcopal Church. Emerging from the Society's tradition of prayer, theological reflection, and diversity of mission, the press is centered in the rich heritage of the Anglican Communion.

Cowley Publications seeks to provide books, audio cassettes, and other resources for the ongoing theological exploration and spiritual development of the Episcopal Church and others in the body of Christ. To this end, it is dedicated to developing a new generation of theological writers, encouraging them to produce timely, creative, and stimulating publications of excellence, and making these publications available widely, reaching both clergy and lay persons.